DEFINITIVE GUIDE TO F&I

MAX ZANAN

ISBN: 978-1-64184-895-4 (Paperback)

ISBN: 978-1-64184-896-1 (Ebook)

FOREWORD

There are very few true 'thought leaders' in the retail automobile industry which is filled with theorists and conceptual thinking and very little real-world experience.

Max Zanan stands out as an individual with been there and done that executive demeanor and street-level experience. So many experts, authors and modern-day gurus in our business are paper-thin, shallow, with little more depth than impressive social media credentials. Max has the aura of success that demands your full attention the moment he begins to speak. In a few minutes you know he's the real deal. He's one of the few persons I seek out when I have a professional question. Every interaction I learn something.

When I heard Max was writing another book, I asked him if he would he please allow me to write the foreword. My only regret is that I ran out of positive adjectives to describe the man and his work. If you are in the Automotive Business, you're going to appreciate this book, and you'll be looking for other things he's written. This is my friend and associate, Max Zanan.

JIM ZIEGLER, CSP, HSG

INTRODUCTION

Thank you for buying this exciting book. You know me as the author of *Perfect Dealership*, *Car Business 101*, *The Art and Science of Running a Car Dealership*, and *Effective Car Dealer*. I wrote these books as a wake-up call for car dealers because if we do not adopt to the new environment, our entire industry might be the next Blockbuster, which failed to upgrade, went bankrupt in 2010 and disappeared completely four years later. New environment means different things at different times. The rise of Carvana, the pandemic, the attacks on the franchise laws by carmakers and the overwhelming growthy of technology are just a few examples of the everchanging competitive landscape.

This book's focus is the Finance and Insurance Department and how the proper management, product selection, and participation structure will positively impact the bottom line. I hope this book will serve as a roadmap for your dealership to maximize every opportunity in the F&I arena and help you stay competitive in such a changing marketplace.

A little bit about me:

I am a seasoned automotive industry professional with more than 20 years of experience in sales, F&I, compliance and dealership consulting. After graduating John Jay (NY) College of Criminal

Justice, I went on to get my master's degree before starting my career in automotive retail as a salesman at a New York City Volkswagen dealership. After working my way up the ranks, I then became the General Manager of a Long Island Mitsubishi dealership, which subsequently placed No. 1 in sales for Mitsubishi in the United States. I went on to become the Platform President at Elite Auto Group, where I oversaw three dealerships with 150 total personnel.

I then transitioned from automotive retail into F&I Products and Training, when I accepted the position of Executive Director with a large, general agency. As Executive Director, I managed the company's two biggest accounts. I started MZ Dealer Services and later Total Dealer Compliance to enhance sales and promote best practices with automotive dealers across the United States. Through my companies, I utilize all the skills I have picked up over the years in order to cohesively mentor dealerships on how to increase revenue and profitability while eliminating non-compliant practices in all departments.

WHO SHOULD READ THIS BOOK?

Every dealer sells F&I products, and most of you understand the importance of the F&I department in terms of its contribution to your bottom line. Unfortunately, F&I is not a regulated profession. That means you don't need any type of state license to practice. As a result, there is very little formal education available. There is plenty of sales training focusing on **how** to sell F&I products along with compliance training. However, the actual **management** of the F&I department, product selection and different types of participation programs are largely ignored. Most dealers, general managers, and finance managers must figure out these aspects in real time, on the job.

This book is written for the senior management team – dealer principal, general manager, finance director and finance manager – so they can improve profitability of their dealership. Setting up the finance department the right way will generate significant profit for the dealership and build generational wealth for the dealer principal. GMs, finance directors and finance managers will benefit from understanding important management practices while the dealer principal will gain an in-depth understanding of various participation programs such as retro and reinsurance as well as a dealer-owned warranty company.

DISCLAIMER

This book does not contain investment advice and does not constitute any offer or solicitation to offer or recommendation of any investment product. It is for general purposes only and does not take into account your individual needs, investment objectives and specific financial circumstances. Every dealership is different. You should consider seeking **independent legal, financial, taxation or other advice** to check how the information in this book relates to your unique circumstances.

PART 1

Brief History of F&I

For more than 100 years, various people and businesses have contributed to the development of the modern dealership's F&I department.

The General Motors Acceptance Corp., established in 1919 thanks to John Raskob's efforts, helped popularize the idea of mass-market consumer financing and set the bar for captive finance businesses. Raskob, considered a financial wizard and also known for building the Empire State Building, served simultaneously as vice president of finance for both DuPont de Nemours and Company and General Motors. In 1919, he revolutionized the auto industry by pioneering automotive credit. For the first time, customers could purchase an automobile on installments directly from dealers.

That required paperwork. When Reynolds and Reynolds Co. agreed to give Chevrolet dealers identical accounting forms in 1927, the company's business of providing dealers with standardized forms took off. It was a significant advancement for Reynolds' automotive industry, but the now 157-year-old business didn't stop there. In the 1960s, it added software to its portfolio of dealership offerings and eventually rose to prominence as a major supplier of dealer management systems and software.

In 1932, Central States Health & Life Co. of Omaha (CSO) opened its doors and began selling the Thrifty plan, a credit life insurance program that assumed responsibility for loan payments for customers who were unable to repay them due to illness or injury. The timing was not fortuitous since the Great Depression was already underway by then, and many people were having trouble repaying car loans. It has long been believed that the "I" in F&I stands for credit life insurance, maybe the first supplementary product sold by car dealers. After more than 80 years in business, CSO is still widely regarded as the industry leader in credit insurance in the U.S. vehicle retail sector.

F&I wasn't far behind. Relying on CSO, Pat Ryan established the first specialized F&I department at Dick Fencl Chevrolet in suburban Chicago in 1962. In the process, he segregated car financing and accessory sales from other operations. He spoke with each client individually and provided financing as well as credit life insurance. Soon after, he began setting up F&I departments at additional dealerships because the approach worked so successfully. In 1964, he started a business to market his services.

Credit Life Insurance

Let's take a deeper dive into credit life insurance since it was the only available product in the beginning stages of F&I. According to Investopedia:

"Credit life insurance is a type of life insurance policy designed to pay off a borrower's outstanding debts if the policyholder dies. It's typically used to ensure you can paydown a large loan like a mortgage or car loan.

The face value of a credit life insurance policy decreases proportionately with the outstanding loan amount as the loan is paid off over time until there is no remaining loan balance."

What is the difference between life insurance and credit life insurance?

In contrast to credit life, which is a straightforward payout by a financial institution to cover existing debt and can be claimed should a customer be permanently disabled, laid off, or die, a life insurance policy typically serves to lessen a family's financial burden after the death of a breadwinner.

History of Factory Warranties

It is also important to understand the history of automobile factory warranties since this history is directly connected to the creation of a vehicle service contract (VSC). Keep in mind, a VSC is the most profitable F&I product.

The familiar maxim *caveat emptor*, "buyer beware," served as the standard during the early years of the automotive age. Cars were a collection of shoddily crafted components produced from dubious materials, with workmanship that varied depending on the day and the supplier. Cars were built one by one and by hand. Consistent quality could not be guaranteed and covered by a defined warranty until Henry Ford introduced the assembly line and supply chains in 1913.

To support his cars, Ford began to offer a standard guarantee, such as this one on a 1925 Model T: 90 days on material; 30 days on labor. However, no guarantee existed for fan belts, glass, bulbs, wiring, transmission bands, hose connections, commutator shells, rollers, spark plugs, or gaskets.

Through the 1950s, the 90-day warranty would survive Henry Ford and become the industry norm. The number of "wear items" that weren't acceptable shrank, but manufacturers still felt there should be a mileage cap, so they set it at 4,000 miles. That's a far cry from the original idea that cars did not last long. The length of the Indianapolis 500 was chosen in 1911 because manufacturers thought 500 miles was the farthest a car could go.

The auto business started to resemble the market we know today by 1960. By then, imports from Europe and Japan began to flood the market, prompting Detroit to release newly designed compact cars.

Factory cash incentives and, more significantly, Ford's comprehensive 1-year/12,000-mile new-car warranty – the longest provided by a mainstream manufacturer – were other breakthroughs of the era. It was quickly surpassed by the 1961 Ford's luxury division Lincoln Continental's 2-year/24,000-mile coverage, which included "associated labor."

By the middle of the 1960s, competition forced the Big Three automakers to extend engine or powertrain coverage up to five years or 50,000 miles. Longer warranties, however, turned out to be expensive for automakers that were still producing low-quality cars.

In response to the rising costs from claims and warranty administration, by the early 1970s, warranties had been reduced to one year. However, consumers had grown to expect such an amenity. That forced Detroit to bring up the issue again after observing the beneficial impact that generous warranties had on auto sales.

Throughout the 1980s, 1990s, and 2000s, factory warranties kept getting longer. These days, we are all familiar with 10 year/100,000-mile warranty offered by Kia and Hyundai or 4 year/50,000 mile warranty offered by virtually every luxury manufacturer.

History of Vehicle Service Contract

Vehicle Service Contract, which made its appearance in the 1970s, is the proper term for the extended warranties. Majority of consumers do not see the distinction between the two and, in most cases, use the term "extended warranty." Before VSC, majority of new cars came with one year/12,000-mile factory warranty. Used cars were sold without a warranty.

Third party administrators (TPA) soon saw an opportunity, and many began offering two- and three-year limited warranties on used vehicles. Over time, TPAs realized that they could expand their product offering by extending factory warranties on new vehicles. Covering new cars was the definition of a cash flow bonanza, as the cost of the VSC was paid upfront while the claims payout only started after the manufacturer's warranty expired. In the early and middle 1980s, interest rates were very high, luring investors with the prospect of big returns.

Manufacturers started launching their own extended warranties, driving independent TPAs out of business or forcing them to lower their prices. Some of these TPAs were backed by insurance companies and survived, but many were not.

Due to horribly inadequate pricing for new vehicle service contracts, this industry experienced turbulence in the late 1980s. During this time, the manufacturers also started to increase the underlying warranty's term to three years or 36,000 miles. This immediately created a pricing issue. Customers who purchased an extended warranty would anticipate a decrease in price since the manufacturer now covered more claims. Actuarial analyses, however, suggested that double-digit rate hikes were required. Also, interest rates were falling, which reduced TPA's income from investing premium dollars.

TPAs that hiked rates saw a significant decline in volume almost immediately as a result of dealers' inability to choose between the products of manufacturers or other independents. Yet, a few independents did make it through this time. It is safe to say that most reputable third-party administrators currently are owned or closely affiliated with large insurance companies, such as Allstate, Zurich, Protective, IA, etc.

Another important point is that, in most states, the extended warranty service contract is not considered insurance and is not regulated by the insurance department. It is simply a contract between the dealer and the car buyer and is covered under contract law. This is the reason why finance managers are allowed to sell vehicle service contracts without becoming licensed insurance brokers.

Since the creation of the F&I department more than 50 years ago, the finance and insurance sector has grown significantly in terms of its ancillary product offerings. As a result, the majority of manufacturers in the captive financing model have adapted to meet the changing needs of consumers and have tightened consumer-protection compliance standards.

What is F&I?

This book will probe the finance department and what it takes to set up a great one. Before we define F&I, we need to understand that the finance department generates the most profit per square foot, and that finance managers are the backbone of a successful dealership.

Here is my definition of a great finance department: an integral part of a car dealership, employing professionals who are tasked with obtaining financing and generating profits through the sale of service contracts and ancillary products, and by marking up interest rates. In addition, the finance department works closely with sales and service department towards a common goal of customer satisfaction and retention. The cherry on top is when the dealer principal sets up a good participation structure that includes a reinsurance or a dealer-owned warranty company (DOWC) in order to build generational wealth on the backend.

Let's dissect this definition and go through it.

First, what is F&I? F&I stands for Finance and Insurance. It is mostly Finance now because car dealers stopped selling Credit Life and Credit Disability Insurance a long time ago due to limited commissions.

Second, what does it do? As mentioned before, F&I is tasked with obtaining financing and generating profits through the sale of service contracts and ancillary products, and by marking up interest rates.

Third, finance department is not a standalone entity. It is an integral part of the overall dealership's operation. To emphasize: it must work closely with sales and service department to ensure customer satisfaction and retention.

Fourth, a participation structure is extremely important to long-term financial growth. The right participation structure will get you there faster.

Finally, what are the risks coming out of the Finance Department? An improperly run Finance Department can cause a tremendous amount of liability in terms of fines, penalties and damage to the dealership's reputation.

What will this book cover?

In this book we will review the following topics:

- Hiring the right finance managers
- Establishing realistic profit expectations and pay plans

- Selecting the right F&I agent
- Selecting the right mix of F&I products
- Benefits of preloaded products
- Training
- F&I and Service Department
- Displaying F&I products on the dealership's website
- Understanding the proper workload
- Menu presentation
- Unsold customer follow-up
- Compliance in F&I department
- Fees charged by third-party administrators
- Different types of participation programs
- Word tracks that work
- Best practices.

Hiring The Right Finance Managers

Let's start with a necessary first step: hiring the ideal finance manager. As you know, talented, customer-focused personnel are the key to success in any business. The following quote is one of the founding principles of The Container Store, one of the most respected and profitable retailers in the country:

"One great person equals three good people. This is our hiring philosophy. Talent is the whole ball game. We're wild-eyed fanatics when it comes to hiring great people. We're constantly on the lookout for amazing employees who elevate the game of everyone around them to a new level."

If you put The Container Store quote in perspective, it means that one great finance manager will be as productive or as effective as the three good finance managers. To attract talent, you should be able to pay them more than the industry average. Just imagine the level of talent your dealership could attract if you paid 20 percent, 30 percent, or even 50 percent more than the competition. Here is another quote from Kip Tindell, the founder of The Container Store:

"Another important aspect of our 1=3 philosophy: Since we're getting at least three times the productivity from our employees (it's a purposeful understatement – you can actually get much, much more than three times the productivity at certain endeavors), we can afford to pay the people closest to the customer – our salespeople – 50 to 100 percent higher than the retail average, to communicate with them breathlessly, and to provide excellent benefits, hundreds of hours of training, and a happy place to go to work every day.

It's a win-win-win.

The employee wins because she's getting paid twice as much and gets to work alongside other great people.

The company wins because it's getting three times the productivity at two times the payroll cost.

And our customers win because they're getting great service from highly motivated employees."

So, what qualifications should you look for when hiring a finance manager?

Let's start with the basics – criminal background checks. Make sure you do them. There is no need to hire people with histories of felonies and misdemeanors. There are plenty of talented people out there. You might even find you already have the right person on your staff already.

Also, consider credit checks. Credit history is a pretty good reflection of character. Plenty of employees use it to make hiring decisions. Insurance companies use credit history when making underwriting decisions. For example, you and I are the same age, live in the same zip code and buy identical cars. Your quote could be significantly less because you have excellent credit history whereas my quote may be much higher because my credit is not so great. Finance managers discuss monthly budgets with customers and need to have a good idea of what it means to budget. Having bad credit is proof that budgeting is not the real strength of a job applicant.

In addition, make sure your dealership requires drug tests. Do not just test for illegal narcotics like cocaine and heroin; test for prescription drugs as well because there is an opioid epidemic in this country. If applicants test positive, ask them to provide a prescription. If they cannot provide a prescription, they may be obtaining these drugs illegally. There is no need to hire a finance manager with a prescription-drug problem. There are plenty of talented people who do not have that liability.

Another best practice is to conduct an asset check on your finance manager and senior management team in general. Discovering that your finance manager is buying a mansion in Beverly Hills or a yacht better raise a red flag.

Once you have completed checks of an applicant's background, possible drug usage and asset, you want to make sure that the applicant has the necessary experience and training. That means checking references. Unfortunately, a lot of car dealers do not check references at all. Here is an interesting statistic from Monster.com:

"***Desperate times often call for desperate measures – and in a brutal employment market, some job seekers may be tempted to falsify their work or education history in order to make themselves more attractive to potential employers. HireRight.com, a provider of on-demand employment background screening, found that 34 percent of job applicants lie on resumes.***"

We live in a litigious society. Often, it may seem pointless to contact previous employers because they will not tell you anything except for the dates of employment. I suggest contacting lenders. Lenders usually are familiar with most finance managers in the area and can tell you if they submit clean deals or engage in credit application falsification, used car power booking, payment packing and jamming of F&I products. We will discuss these non-compliant and unethical practices in the Compliance section of this book.

During the interview with an applicant, you want to find out what back-end gross profit the applicant was generating at his previous employer. If the answer seems unrealistic – for example, $3,500 per copy – that is not because the applicant is that good but because he/she may have been lying and misleading customers. Steer clear.

Another best practice is to ask the applicant to go through an entire sales presentation. A true professional will be able to do just that with no hesitation.

You also want to make sure that the applicant understands the importance of compliance and has previous compliance training and certification. The Association of Finance and Insurance Professionals provides very thorough certification that covers federal and state-specific regulations as well as ethics. My company, Total Dealer Compliance, also offers extensive online training for new hires and existing employees.

What type of culture does your dealership have?

Once you decide to hire a particular individual, you must explain the culture of your organization and what behavior is not going to be tolerated. In order to avoid misunderstandings in the future, your dealership's policy and procedures must be clearly spelled out and in writing. Each new hire should sign off on understanding these policies as well as the consequences for breaking them. For example, you might have a "one strike and you're out" policy for falsifying credit applications. This policy means that falsifying credit applications will result in immediate termination of employment. Make sure to enforce the policies you have created. If you don't, your employees will habitually break them. Your dealership will suffer as a result.

A clear job description is the key. This may seem elementary, but it is not. The concept is foundational and works to both define and align operations throughout the organization.

Effective staff development is based on clear job descriptions. This approach will help avoid confusion when it comes to responsibilities. In many instances during my career, I have seen dealerships where there is no unequivocal definition who is supposed to perform a particular function. Moreover, most dealerships do not have written job descriptions at all.

That can lead to lost income. For example, who follows up with customers who declined to purchase F&I products – the F&I department or the BDC department? Clear job descriptions eliminate any confusion.

Having an effective onboarding process is important for any successful organization. Please check out our library of online courses designed for all employees of a car dealership.

Realistic Profit Expectations

What can you expect to earn from your F&I Department? In 2012, a study by Zurich found that the average F&I profit per retail unit was less than $800, although top performers averaged more than $1,100 per retail unit. That's increased over time as shown by looking what publicly owned auto groups were averaging in F&I in 2022. Below are the numbers produced by six publicly held auto groups. Five out of the six largest publicly traded auto dealer groups average more than $2,000 in F&I profit per vehicle in the second quarter of that year.

	Q2 2022	Q2 2021	Change
Asbury	$ 2,409.00	1,830.00	32%
Penske	$ 1,951.00	1,604.00	22%
Group 1	$ 2,504.00	2,115.00	18%
AutoNation	$ 2,720.00	2,340.00	16%
Sonic	$ 2,440.00	2,113.00	15%
Lithia	$ 2,146.00	1,875.00	14%

This is a good industry benchmark to target. Back-end profit is made up of finance reserve and upsell of F&I products such as service contracts, GAP and key replacement, among other items.

Product Penetration

To achieve that level, you need to achieve certain product penetration. To begin with, your dealership needs to decide what products count towards penetration. For example, you can only count paper products such as service contracts, pre-paid maintenance, etc., or you can also include accessories. Once you determine what products count towards penetration, then you need to look at historical data going back at least 12 months to determine existing product penetration.

When that study is complete, you are ready to set a realistic product penetration requirement and then start slowly raising it. For example, you might start out at 125 percent (1.25 products per deal) and slowly start raising it 5 percent until you get to 175 percent to 200 percent. F&I incentives, better known as spiffs, will help drive the point home. I work with many dealerships where finance managers forfeit the spiffs if they don't hit the target penetration.

To reduce cancelations and customer complaints, I recommend setting a maximum selling price for each product. Absence of a maximum sale price allows a finance manager to sell less products at a higher margin. Properly managed finance departments generate more product sales at lower margins because their goal is to create value for each customer. For example, a $450 mark-up on each F&I product means that a finance manager will have to sell three products per customer to average $1,350 and generate another $750 from the finance reserve. This approach prevents price gouging.

Better yet, I suggest you go to a one-price model for all F&I products. You could still discount, but this approach ensures you offer your products at the same price to 100 percent of your customers. There is no reason for customer A to pay more for an identical product compared to customer B.

Pay Plans

Your dealership has to design easily understandable salary plans. Nobody likes changes in pay, and employees at a dealership are no different. Unfortunately, it has become almost a standard operating procedure for dealer principals repeatedly to change pay plans. This is demoralizing and unacceptable, and it leads to employee turnover and dissatisfaction.

The HR director together with senior management need to design clear and easily understandable pay plans and bonus plans for all employees, and stick to them.

I am big fan of motivational pay plans that pay on both product penetration and gross profit. In addition, I would add additional points for excellent customer service and timely funding of deals. As I mentioned in the beginning of the book, you should happily overpay great employees.

For example, in New York City, finance managers get paid between 13 and 18 percent of sales, and good ones get 20 percent. Just imagine what kind of talent your dealership could attract if you were willing to pay 25 percent or even 30 percent. Just imagine the reduction in personnel turnover that kind of bonus would lead to.

The higher pay is offset by the savings. According to Forbes, for decades, experts in talent management have emphasized the extra costs resulting from employee turnover. It is usually said that depending upon the complexity of the job and the level of management, the cost of turnover can equal anywhere from one month's to several years' salary for a departing employee. The more complex the job and the higher level of the job, the greater the cost.

The costs associated with turnover often lead to recommendations that organizations should monitor turnover and reduce it to a "minimum." The best ways to accomplish that is by paying higher wages, creating a satisfied workforce.

In addition, employees that are paid more than their peers in other organizations value the job much more and almost invariably strive to exceed dealer expectations. Remember that pay plans drive behavior.

Another way to stimulate product penetration and provide an additional opportunity for finance managers to make extra income is to pay incentives for each product sold. Or you can set up a floating incentive: that's an incentive that is paid on a particular product for a set period. This approach ensures that every product gets its fair share in the presentation.

Throughout the years of dealing with car dealers, I have found that they tend to fall into two categories. First category believes in paying spiffs to finance managers while the other category doesn't. I have never seen much success at dealerships relying on the second category. Their philosophy is counterproductive to efforts to increase product penetration and gross profit.

The main takeaways here are that it is to your advantage to overpay for talent and to use extra income as incentive.

Selecting The Right F&I Agent

Now let's shift our focus and discuss F&I agents. Every dealership works with an F&I agent. This section is dedicated to choosing the right one. The F&I agent should be an integral part of a successful finance department.

There are three types of F&I agents: big box companies such as JM&A and Zurich; Original Equipment Manufacturers (OEM)-labeled programs; and smaller, independent general agents.

Companies such as JM&A and Zurich invariably make a strong impression when they fly in six guys in suits. Unfortunately, you probably won't see them ever again. Dealers usually end up being serviced by inexperienced account reps who regularly get promoted or reassigned to a different territory. Therefore, there is rarely any continuity, although there are sky-high admin fees.

Original Equipment Manufacturers (OEMs) such as Nissan recognize that F&I is a great way to generate additional revenue. They aggressively market F&I products to their dealers. Keep in mind that OEMs do not have in-house F&I products or trainers. They white label their products by using third-party administrators such as Safeguard, Allstate, etc. OEMs incentivize dealers through additional trunk money and reduced interest rates on the floor plan. Some go as far as advance hundreds of thousands of dollars that must be repaid through the sale of OEM-branded F&I products.

Lately, I see OEMs using another trick to convince dealers to sell their F&I products. They advance more for their products versus third-party products. Some OEMs offer dealers participation structures, such as reinsurance. They entice dealers to participate by promising better allocations. I think the COVID-related inventory shortages completely busted that myth.

I have been doing F&I consulting for many years and can say with certainty that OEMs do not have the necessary expertise. F&I is not just about products but also about training and motivating. Not to mention that every OEM-branded product is more expensive than a third-party solution because of a much more liberal claims-adjudication process. Think about it: how could third-party F&I product providers stay in business if their products were more expensive than the OEM offering?

In my experience, third-party solutions coupled with an effective general agent will always produce better results.

Smaller independent agents also fall into two categories. The first category is what I call "accidental agents." They became agents by accident because they are friends with the dealer principal. In most cases, these guys have never worked in the car business and really don't understand it. Therefore, they can't provide quality training or bring income-development ideas to the table.

The second category is a tiny minority, but these guys really know what they are doing. Working with them can make a huge difference. I am proud to be in this category. They have prior dealership experience as GMs or directors of finance, and they understand the business. They will provide quality training, set benchmarks and hold finance managers accountable, and bring excellent income-development solutions as well as help the dealership implement them. Experienced agents will make sure that F&I products are approved by state insurance departments and that they are underwritten by reputable A-rated insurance companies. Most importantly, they will help the dealer principal choose the right participation model in order to build generational wealth.

When selecting the right F&I agent, dealers should make sure that the vendor has prior automotive retail management experience, compliance certification and quality references. At the very minimum, I recommend that F&I providers be Automotive Finance and Insurance Professional (AFIP) certified. AFIP certification is not easy to achieve as it requires many hours of self-study, a boot camp and a three-hour test that covers federal and state regulations as well as ethics.

I strongly suggest that dealer principals really examine and assess who their F&I agents are and what they do for them.

If you have any questions regarding F&I training, products, and income development do not hesitate to reach out to me and go to my website www.maxzanan.com

Selecting The Right Mix of F&I Products

What kind of F&I products should your dealership carry? Here are the most essential products that every dealership should offer customers:

- Vehicle Service Contracts
- Limited Powertrain Warranty
- Gap Insurance
- Tire and Wheel Protection
- Paint & Fabric Protection
- Key Replacement
- Lease Wear & Tear
- Total Term Protection
- Paintless Dent Repair
- Antitheft Protection
- LoJack type of security device
- Combo (for example, tire and wheel, key replacement, paintless dent repair and roadside assistance, or any combination of ancillary products).
- Prepaid maintenance.

Let's review each product in detail.

Vehicle Service Contracts

A Vehicle Service Contract (VSC), which was introduced earlier, is the ultimate profit generator in the F&I department. It is also a primary wealth builder in any participation program, such as reinsurance or a dealer-owned warranty company.

A VSC comes in two forms: Dealer Obligor and Admin Obligor contracts. It is important to understand the difference between them. While the actual mechanics of the program will be somewhat similar, under Dealer Obligor, your dealership bears the responsibility for all the obligations to the consumer, including financial responsibility for the payment of claims. With an Admin Obligor contract, you're transferring your obligations to a third party. My suggestion is to stay away from Dealer Obligor contracts unless you have an incredible financial discipline. More on this later in this book.

VSCs come in two flavors: Exclusionary and Stated Component Coverage. Exclusionary coverage covers any vehicle part experiencing a mechanical breakdown before the mechanical coverage expires or is canceled except for the parts listed in "Exclusions and Other Coverage Limitations." This is what most finance managers **incorrectly** refer to as "bumper-to-bumper coverage or Platinum coverage."

Stated Component covers any part specifically stated. These vehicle service contracts usually have different tiers: Gold, Silver and Bronze.

Bronze coverage or powertrain coverage usually covers the following:

Gasoline/Diesel engine: all internal lubricated parts • engine block • cylinder heads • harmonic balancer • manifold(s): exhaust/ intake (excluding catalytic converters) • oil pan (excluding drain plug related failures) • oil pump • electric oil pump • timing belt/chain, gear, cover and tensioner • manufacturer-installed turbocharger(s) • manufacturer-installed supercharger • valve covers.

Transmission (Automatic, continuous variable (CVT), standard and transfer case): all internal lubricated parts • transmission and transfer case housing • torque converter • mounts • flywheel/ flexplate • vacuum modulator • electric oil pump.

Drive axle (Front/Rear/AWD/4-wheel drive): all internal lubricated parts within the drive/transaxle assembly and housing, including axles and axle bearings • hubs, bearings and front hub locking assemblies • constant velocity joints • universal joints • drive shaft • locking rings • wheel bearings.

Cooling/Fuel: thermostat/housing • water pump/housing • electric coolant pump • throttle body assembly • diesel accessory vacuum pump, injectors and injection pump • fuel pump.

Hybrid vehicle: hybrid vehicle electric motor assembly • electronic transmission/transaxle assembly • electric traction-drive motor assembly.

Filters, fluids, lubricants and taxes: filters, fluids, lubricants and taxes required to complete a covered repair for any covered part listed.

Seals and gaskets: Seals and gaskets for all covered parts listed.

Silver coverage includes all items listed under Bronze coverage plus the following:

Transmission (automatic, continuous variable (CVT), standard and transfer case).

Cooling/Fuel: radiator fan relay • fuel lines.

Air conditioning: compressor: clutch, coil and electric engine • pulleys and bearings • pressure cycling switch • dash control unit / temperature control module • condenser • evaporator • dye, flushing liquids or refrigerant(s) if needed in conjunction with a covered repair.

Brakes: backing plates • disc brake calipers • wheel cylinders • master and power brake cylinder • vacuum assist booster • hydraulic lines / fittings • manual or electronic parking brake system and cables (excluding handle).

Electrical: alternator and voltage regulator • ignition module • ignition coils • switches/buttons including manually or mechanically operated electrical switches • starter motor, solenoid and starter drive • wiper motors • wiring harnesses for electrical covered parts.

Steering: all internal lubricated parts within the steering gear and power steering pump • control valve • power steering lines, hoses, cooler and couplings • tie rod ends • idler arm • pitman arm •

intermediate and main shaft • drag link • rack-and-pinion gear and housing • steering knuckle • electric power steering system.

Suspension: ball joints • control arms, shafts and bushings • linkage and bushings • struts, mounts and bushings • stabilizer bar, links and bushings • spindle/spindle support.

Seals and gaskets: Seals and gaskets for all covered parts listed.

Gold coverage includes all items listed under Silver and Bronze coverage plus the following:

Gasoline/Diesel engine: oil pressure sending unit • mounts.

Transmission (Automatic, continuous variable (CVT), standard and transfer case): transmission cooler/metal lines • transmission range sensor • external transmission solenoids.

Cooling/Fuel: mass air flow sensors/meters • oxygen sensors • fuel tank • fuel tank sending unit • radiator • blade assembly and fan clutch • electric cooling fan motor.

Air conditioning: accumulator • receiver/dryer • temperature control actuators and motors • thermostatic expansion valve • blower motor and resistor • heater core • lines and hoses • belt tensioner.

Brakes: antilock brake system • brake pedal shaft.

Steering: column lock • tilt wheel mechanism.

Suspension: electronic level control system.

Electrical: control modules: body, cruise, engine, powertrain, transmission and wiper • motors: convertible top, door lock, mirror, seat track, sunroof and window • window regulator • door lock actuators • sensors: camshaft position, coolant temperature, crankshaft angle and throttle position • instrument cluster • keyless entry system • rear window defroster (electrical failures only) • radio • compact disc player • wiring harnesses for electrical covered parts.

Seals and gaskets: Seals and gaskets for all covered parts listed.

Most vehicle service contracts come with these additional benefits, such as:

Road service allowance

Reimbursement of up to $100 of coverage per incident for emergency roadside assistance expenses incurred for the following:

- Towing or winch-out service
- Battery assistance – excluding hybrid vehicle main power cell batteries
- Flat tire assistance – with vehicle's inflated spare
- Fuel, water or other fluid delivery – excluding the cost of fluids
- Lock-out assistance.

Substitute transportation

Reimbursement of up to $35 per day, for a maximum of 7 days per occurrence, for expenses incurred to rent a substitute vehicle from a licensed rental car agency or for public or private commercial transportation while the vehicle is undergoing a covered repair.

Trip interruption

Reimbursement for meals and lodging up to $100 per day for a maximum of three days when the vehicle is undergoing a covered repair due to a mechanical breakdown that has occurred more than 100 miles from the customer's residence and the repair facility keeps the vehicle overnight.

Transferable and cancelable – subject to fees

Also, most vehicle service contracts offer the following optional coverages.

Lift kit / tire modifications

Covers eligible vehicles with an aftermarket, manufacturer and/or dealer installed suspension alteration parts, non-OEM tire modifications and/ or lift kits with no more than a 6" suspension lift or a

3" suspension drop from the OEM specifications and/or non-OEM tires that do not exceed the OEM specifications by more than 4" in diameter.

Snowplow

Covers eligible vehicles with less than a three-quarter ton rating that are equipped with a manufacturer snowplow package, including a snowplow prep package. The snowplow itself, all of its assembly and any aftermarket and/ or manufacturer or dealer-installed snowplow accessories and /or equipment are not covered. The vehicle must be used for personal use only. Cannot be combined with Business Use Coverage.

Business use

Covers eligible vehicles with less than one-ton rating, used solely or partially in pursuit of a business or for the generation of income, regardless of whether the vehicle is registered to an individual or business. Cannot be combined with the snowplow coverage.

If the dealership is looking to improve customer satisfaction and reduce cancellations, then offer the Exclusionary coverage, which means that the finance manager doesn't have to deal with an irate customer because a particular repair wasn't covered.

Limited Powertrain Warranty

It is important to understand the difference between a VSC contracts and limited warranties.

A VSC is similar to an extended warranty and can be purchased when the customer buys a used or new vehicle or for a car that the customer already owns, as long as it's an eligible make and model.

On the other hand, a limited warranty cannot be purchased. It must be included in the price of the car, akin to a new car factory warranty. For example, when you purchase a new car, the factory warranty is included in the price so the customer cannot be charged for it. Limited Powertrain Warranty is a short-term warranty (3/6/12 months) that is offered by a car dealer on all the used cars in stock. Usually this is done for three reasons:

- To enhance the Why Buy from Us story
- To have the reserves earn out quickly in the dealer's reinsurance company
- Easier upsell to the VSC.

Let me elaborate on these three points. First, if you decide to offer a limited powertrain warranty on all used cars in stock, then make sure to make this fact known. Turn it into a marketing campaign. Make sure that there are web banners on your website and marketing materials in the showroom. The name of the game is to stand out from the completion.

Second, short-term, limited warranties earn out quickly, and the claims are low, assuming that your dealership does a good job reconditioning cars. Quick earnout means you are building reserves quickly in your reinsurance or dealer-owned warranty company.

Third, it is much easier for the finance manager to upsell to the full vehicle-service contract. Once customers understand that only three components are covered – engine, transmission, and drive axle – they realize the need to protect the remaining parts.

Limited Powertrain Warranty

A limited powertrain warranty provides customers the peace of mind knowing that they are protected against the cost of covered breakdowns. When customers buy a vehicle from your dealership, they can be assured that the vehicle has protection against mechanical failure.

A limited powertrain warranty covers the following parts within these important component groups:

Gasoline/diesel engine: all internal lubricated parts • engine block • cylinder heads • harmonic balancer • manifold(s) exhaust/intake (excluding catalytic converters) • oil pan (excluding drain plug related failures) • electric oil pump • fuel pump • timing belt/ chain, gear, cover and tensioner • water pump • electric coolant pump • diesel accessory vacuum pump, lift pump, injectors and injector pump • pulleys: timing belt and crankshaft • manufacturer-installed turbo-charger(s), bypass valve(s), blow-off valve(s), intercooler and waste gate(s) • manufacturer-installed supercharger • valve covers.

Transmission (Automatic, Continuous Variable (CVT), Standard and Transfer Case)**:** all internal lubricated parts • transmission and transfer case housing • transmission cooler • metal cooler lines • oil pan (excluding drain plug related failures) • torque converter • mounts • flywheel/flexplate • oil pump • throttle valve cable • vacuum modulator • external and internal control unit • automatic electronic clutches.

Drive Axle (Front/Rear/AWD/4-Wheel Drive): all internal lubricated parts within the drive/transaxle assembly and housing, including axles and axle bearings • hubs, bearings and front hub locking assemblies • constant velocity joints • universal joints • drive shaft • differential cover • four-wheel drive actuator.

Hybrid Vehicle: hybrid vehicle electric motor assembly • electronic transmission/transaxle assembly • electric traction-drive motor assembly.

Filters, Fluids, Lubricants and Taxes: filters, fluids, lubricants and taxes required to complete a covered repair for any covered part listed above.

Seals and Gaskets: Seals and gaskets for all covered parts listed above when subject to a covered repair.

Gap Insurance

This Guaranteed Auto Protection insurance kicks in in when a car is totaled or stolen. Harking back to the initial insurance plans, Gap insurance pays any money you owe on the car that exceeds the insurance payout from your comprehensive or collision coverage. While the insurance is not required in all states, most insurers require drivers carry comprehensive and collision coverage, so gap insurance can be very valuable if a vehicle is totaled before being paid off. Studies show that new vehicles in their first year typically lose about 30 percent of their value and 20 percent in the second year. As a result, car owners could end up owing more than their car is worth if it is damaged or stolen. Gap insurance provides the additional funds.

Gap Coverage highlights:

- Payable in the event of a total loss
- Covers the difference, in most cases, between the scheduled assets
- Pay-off amount net of refunds and the asset's actual cash value
- Also covers primary insurance deductible up to $1,000
- Gap coverage remains intact if primary automotive insurance coverage lapses
- Gap benefit covers up to $50,000
- Coverage available for most financed new and pre-owned vehicles.

Tire and Wheel Protection

Tire and wheel protection normally comes in three choices – Tire Plan, Tire and Wheel Plan, and Tire and Wheel Plan with Cosmetic Coverage.

Tire Plan

The Tire Plan covers the repair, or, if unrepairable, the replacement of tires damaged by road hazards. Coverage includes mounting, balancing, wheel weights, valve stems, patches/patch plugs and taxes required to complete a covered repair.

Tire & Wheel Plan

In addition to the tire coverage, the Tire & Wheel Plan covers the repair or replacement of wheels damaged by road hazards.

Tire & Wheel Plan with Cosmetic Repair

The Tire & Wheel Plan with Cosmetic Repair covers the tires, wheels and appearance of wheels damaged by a road hazard. Coverage includes the repair of abrasions, scuffs, scratches or scrapes to wheels that are caused by a road hazard.

Paint and Fabric Protection

Exterior - paint sealant.

Completely seals and protects paint.

Rip and tear protection

Protect against permanent damage to the interior of your vehicle, weather-induced or ultraviolet-induced weakening resulting in fading, cracking, loose stitching, rips or tears less than 2 inches, or punctures less than 1/4 inch in diameter.

Interior - fabric, carpet, leather and vinyl

Seals out water and oil-based stains. Protects from premature aging and makes clean-up easy.

Covered stain-causing items include:

- Food
- Drink
- Vomit

- Urine
- Pet stains
- Gum
- Crayons
- Ink
- Dyes
- Lipstick
- Makeup
- Blood
- Baby diapers
- Topical oils /lotions.

Additional features and benefits

- Substitute Transportation: Up to $35 per day for up to 3 days
- Contract is transferable to a private party purchaser if the customer sells the vehicle while the contract is still in force, which may add to resale value – in accordance with rules for transfer procedures and pay transfer fee.

Key repair & replacement

Repair or replacement of vehicle key(s)/ remote(s) lost, stolen, damaged or destroyed, including any applicable programming. Coverage is limited to $800 per covered repair or replacement and one key/ remote replacement every 12 months.

Protection for other keys

Up to $250 per covered repair or replacement to replace non-programmable keys lost, stolen, damaged or destroyed.

Additional benefits

Towing and lock-out allowance

Reimbursement of up to $100 per occurrence for towing and/or lock-out expenses if a customer 's vehicle becomes inoperable or the customer is locked out of the vehicle, due to vehicle keys/remotes being lost, stolen, damaged or destroyed, or locked inside of the vehicle – regardless of whether it results in a covered repair or replacement. This allowance includes reimbursement for expenses incurred by having a vehicle towed to a repair facility and/or obtaining assistance to unlock the vehicle. Towing and lock-out allowance is available in the United States, its territories and possessions and Canada. Customers must make their own arrangements for towing and lock-out assistance.

Substitute transportation

Customers will be reimbursed up to $50 per day, for a maximum of 2 days per occurrence, for expenses incurred to rent a substitute vehicle from a licensed rental car agency or for public or private commercial transportation if the customer has a covered repair or replacement and is not able to repair or replace the vehicle keys/remotes and drive the vehicle on the same day as the vehicle keys/remotes are lost, stolen, damaged or destroyed. Customers must make their own arrangements for substitute transportation.

Excess Wear and Tear

Leased Vehicle Excess Wear & Tear is designed to cover unexpected wear and tear charges at the end of the lease. Normally, Excess Wear & Tear contracts are not designed to cover the actual repairs. They are designed to reimburse the customer or the financial institution (leasing company) for the wear and tear charges. This product is very popular in the areas with high-lease penetration, such as Northeast, where the leasing penetration can be as high as 95 percent, depending on the brand.

Leased Vehicle Excess Wear & Tear may waive up to $5,000 or $7,500 for excess wear and tear repairs to the following parts:

- Tires
- Paint
- Exterior dents and dings
- Windshield and glass
- Headlamps, tail lamps, light bulbs
- Bumpers, step bumpers, surrounding trim
- Wheels and wheel covers
- Factory audio equipment
- Convertible, padded and vinyl tops
- Upholstery and interior
- Carpets
- Truck bed liners
- Rubber door seals
- Mirrors
- Name plate badges and hood ornaments
- Door handles
- Moldings, trim, metal, chrome
- Belts and hoses.

Finance managers must be well versed in this product.

Total Term Protection

This coverage is specifically designed for leased vehicles.

Covered parts:

- Belt and hose replacements

- Battery replacement
- Brake pad replacement
- Electrical coverage of fuses and lighting
- Headlight bulb replacement
- Fluid replacement with a covered repair.

Covered services:

- Wheel alignment
- Windshield wiper blade replacement.

To be successful in a high-lease penetration area, a finance manager must completely know this product as well.

Theft Deterrent

Theft Deterrent, better known as "window etch," has been around for a long time. Oftentimes, this product is considered controversial since rogue finance managers tend to overcharge for it, negating the product's benefit.

Theft Deterrent Protection Product and Limited Warranty utilizes a unique and traceable vehicle identifier that can be used by law enforcement agencies to provide 24-hour daily protection to help recover a customer's vehicle if it is stolen.

Coverage includes:

- 24 hours a day protection
- $3,000 or $5,000 coverage
- Terms of 3 or 5 years
- May reduce car insurance premium
- Transferable to private party purchaser.

Additional benefits

- **Towing allowance**

  If the vehicle is stolen and recovered within 30 days and is towed to a towing recovery lot, a customer will be reimbursed up to $50 per incident for any towing assistance expenses incurred.

- **Substitute transportation**

  When a vehicle is stolen, a customer will be reimbursed up to $35 per day, for a maximum of 20 days, for expenses incurred to rent a substitute vehicle from a licensed rental car agency or for public or private commercial transportation.

- **Trip interruption**

  Customers will be reimbursed for expenses incurred for meals and lodging up to $100 per day for a maximum of 3 days or up to $300 for one-way public or private commercial transportation back to their primary residence if the vehicle is stolen and the theft occurs more than 100 miles from that primary residence.

- **Homeowner's or renter's insurance deductible**

  Customers will be reimbursed up to $500 for homeowner's or renter's insurance policy deductible if their personal property is stolen from their vehicle on the date of loss.

- **Primary automobile insurance carrier deductible**

  Customers will be reimbursed up to $500 for their primary automobile insurance carrier insurance policy deductible if the vehicle is stolen and recovered within 30 days and the vehicle incurs damage covered by the insurance policy issued by the customer's primary automobile insurance carrier.

Anti-theft/Lot Management Device

There are many anti-theft/lot management devices on the market but from the marketing perspective, there is an undisputed leader

– LoJack, a GPS-connected system that uses a vehicle's VIN number and other details registered with the National Crime Information Center database. The signal reaches 3 to 5 miles and helps law enforcement quickly locate a stolen vehicle. The company claims a 90 percent success rate compared to 12 percent for vehicles without LoJack. The system does not work in the few areas where there's no GPS.

In addition, lot management is a useful tool for vehicles in stock. It allows the dealer to track exact position of the car, battery life, geofence parameters for test drives, etc.

Once the vehicle is sold, these benefits are transferred to the customer. There is also an theft policy that could be attached. In case of the car is stolen and not recovered, a customer will receive $5,000 or $10,000.

Catalytic Converter Etch

Occasionally, there is a new product on the market as part of the industry response to current events. For example, there is a surge of stolen catalytic converters across the country. The cause of the thefts is the same explanation behind such crimes – money. The rhodium, palladium and platinum used in these parts are valuable. For example, rhodium can go for $20,000 per ounce, according to the National Insurance Crime Bureau. I encourage dealers to keep their finger on the pulse and offer products that resonate with consumers. Catalytic converter etch is exactly that.

Combo

Combo is a popular F&I product that combines several ancillary products, such as tire and wheel protection, paintless dent repair, key replacement, and roadside assistance. Instead of pitching each product separately, a finance manager can present a combo in order to offer more value to a customer.

Prepaid Maintenance

There are two types of the prepaid maintenance – factory branded and dealership branded. Factory-branded prepaid maintenance allows the customer to go to any dealership to perform prepaid maintenance. For example, if you are a Honda dealer and sell Honda prepaid maintenance, your customer can go to any Honda dealership to do the work. This is particularly helpful for customers whose vehicle needs maintenance when far from home.

Dealer-branded prepaid maintenance is much more beneficial to you because the customer must come back to your dealership to do the work. This approach increases service retention, and your dollars per repair order eventually will go up as well. As customers are coming back to the dealership for their schedule maintenance, service advisors build a relationship with each customer. Down the road, this relationship makes it easier to upsell additional repair work.

Another advantage of the dealer-branded prepaid maintenance program is that the dealership is in total control when it comes to the design of the program. For example, dealer can decide on the number of oil changes, tire rotations, car washes, etc. As a result, there is more flexibility in comparison with the factory program.

Another critical point is the customer follow up. A dealer-branded program has the customer follow-up built in. Follow up is handled by a third party and consists of emails, text messages, and phone calls. Keep in mind that the factory program has no follow up because the factory is not interested in driving the customer back to the selling dealer because of breakage.

Breakage refers to the premium dollars allocated to prepaid maintenance that are not used. If the customer purchases the factory program and doesn't have any repair work done at the dealership, then the factory keeps the breakage. Guess who keeps the breakage if the customer purchases the dealer-branded program? You guessed it – the selling dealer.

Increasing Service Retention via Tiebacks and Disappearing Deductible

These are retention-based products and require customers to come back to the selling dealer for repairs. Tieback is an excellent strategy because it requires customers to come back to the selling dealer service department for all repairs as long as the breakdown is within a predefined radius – typically within 50 or 75 miles of the selling dealership or if the repair exceeds $1,000.

This approach is a great way to control claims. Once you form a reinsurance company or a dealer-owned warranty company (DOWC), you would want to control claims, since every dollar that you pay out in claims will reduce your underwriting profit. Tiebacks also help with loading the shop. Every dealer principal wants his techs turning wrenches and not hanging out waiting for a flatbed to pull in. Most importantly, when the selling dealer does the work, he is in complete control of the customer experience. Selling dealers could waive a deductible, arrange a loaner vehicle, and even trade the customer out. Ultimately, service retention and service satisfaction is what sells the next car.

A "disappearing deductible" is another great strategy to ensure that customers come back to the selling dealer service department. Basically, there is no deductible if the customer comes back to the selling dealer vs. a $200 or $300 deductible if the customer goes somewhere else.

Finance managers with excellent product knowledge will be able to explain to the customer the beauty of a disappearing deductible.

Preload Programs to Enhance the "Why Buy from Us" Story

Now that you understand what F&I products are available, let's shift gears and talk about preloading and upselling F&I products.

In order to improve your dealership's bottom line and remain relevant in the digital age, it is important to consider two main factors: how to set yourself apart from the competition; and where to focus specifically on increasing profit margins.

When devising a solid strategy to accomplish these objectives, it's crucial to identify universal trends in consumers' retail preferences and align your dealership's sales techniques. Management must also continually think creatively to develop tactics that position its salespeople and inventory most optimally in the eyes of their customers.

Preloaded products make your inventory more appealing and valuable while making the job of salespeople easier. For example, it is easier to build value in a car that comes with preloaded paint and fabric protection and/or 1 year of prepaid maintenance.

The Value of Preinstalled Add-Ons

This is not an easy task, but to be successful, every dealership must find a way to address and conquer challenges posed by modern technology. One way to achieve increased income is by preinstalling low-cost items that are perceived by consumers as high value and positioning them as complimentary add-ons. These items include:

- Dealer-branded prepaid maintenance, which guarantees a customer will come back to the selling dealer's service department to perform scheduled maintenance. What's more, this maintenance plan can only be used at the selling dealer, unlike OEM prepaid maintenance, which can be used at any dealership
- Exterior paint protection, which helps keep the car looking new and increases its trade-in value
- Antitheft protection, which is valuable because car theft is still a prevalent crime in many areas
- Short-term combo product, such as 6 months or 1 year.

The Importance of Upselling

Additionally, to offset the cost of the preload, a dealership's F&I department must be able to upsell the exterior paint protection, prepaid maintenance, and a short-term combo to longer terms and antitheft protection for a greater dollar benefit amount. To do so, a dealership's senior management team should set a certain upsell penetration requirement to incentivize its sales teams.

Adding these items to an overall comprehensive sales strategy will undoubtedly create a sense of loyalty, cultivate a more positive opinion of the dealership and improve profit margins.

Draw Attention to the Add-Ons

Dealers should also be sure to display prominently the items they are including in the sale price of the car on a separate addendum sticker. Sales staff should be trained accordingly and fully understand the value added by these products to better position them with customers.

The information featured on the addendum stickers should also be included in a dealership's print and online efforts – website, TV, radio, Internet, and social media. There should also be marketing materials on every salesperson's desk to reinforce the message. The key here is that online and in-showroom marketing messaging remain consistent.

Dealerships cannot implement a one-size-fits-all approach, however. The items mentioned here are just a few examples of the types of innovations that dealerships could implement in order to stay competitive in the ever-changing marketplace. With dealerships rushing to stand out, many implement tactics without properly validating their customers' needs first, leading to hit-or-miss results. By focusing on benefits as universal as these added perks and low-cost items, dealerships enhance the probability of success.

Often the car sales' process begins online, but there is still a strong need for brick-and-mortar auto dealerships. By showcasing new, innovative ways to stay competitive, dealerships can adapt to changing customer needs and improve their bottom line. It is a good idea to reinsure the preloaded products because of tax advantages and reduction in commissionable gross profit.

Benefits of Preloads from the Reinsurance Perspective

When I mention preloads to dealer principals, they are often categorically opposed because they see preloads as additional cost. They are not wrong; however, once they see the benefits of reinsurance, they become huge fans of preloading F&I products. At the beginning of each month, accounting department must pay for all F&I products sold or preloaded during the previous month. If the dealer is not reinsured, then the cost of the preload turns into extra expense. Once dealers form a reinsurance or dealer- owned warranty company, they mail the checks to their own companies. In other words, they transfers money from the right pocket to the left pocket. This approach allows the dealer to artificially increase expenses in the dealership while decreasing commissionable gross profit. At the same time, of course, the dealer is building reserves in his reinsurance company.

Training in F&I

All general managers and dealer principals understand the importance of training. A majority of dealerships devote every Saturday morning to training their sales teams, focusing on such areas as product knowledge, vehicle walkaround and techniques for overcoming objections.

For some reason, I see way less F&I training compared to sales training although F&I training is readily available from multiple sources.

For example, there are independent F&I trainers such as Jim Ziegler and Reahard and Associates. They have built their careers by training finance managers across the country and are not affiliated with any third-party administrators. In other words, they teach how to sell F&I products in general, not products from a particular vendor.

In addition, there are F&I trainers that work for third-party administrators. For example, if your dealership sells Assurant or Allstate F&I products, you must make sure that they send their trainers to improve the product knowledge of the products that your dealership sells. They can also help with menu presentation and overcoming objections.

Good F&I agents also provide excellent and consistent training. The key word here is **good**. Make sure to set your training expectations when selecting an F&I agent.

Finally, there are training programs offered by majority of state dealer associations as well as the National Automobile Dealers Association. Make sure to take advantage of these opportunities.

There are different delivery methods – online, in-dealership, off-premises. Let's examine each in greater detail.

Online training was not available when I was coming up in the business but is commonplace now. I find it incredibly effective. There are two types of online training. One option provides prerecorded courses on different topics, such as menu presentation, product knowledge and overcoming objections. The alternative is personalized online training. Basically, it is a one-on-one zoom call where the trainer can address concerns of a finance manager. For example, if a finance manager's product penetration of tire and wheel protection is low, the trainer can focus on a manager's presentation skills, product knowledge, etc.

On-line programs do have another advantage. In-dealership training remains the most common training method, but is the least effective because there are endless distractions in the dealership. Finance managers must get deals approved, packaged and funded. They also must deal with customer complaints and cancelations. In other words, in-dealership training session is guaranteed to be interrupted constantly. As a result, very little often can be accomplished.

Some dealerships have countered this by having two sessions. That way some salesmen and a finance manager are waiting on customers while the rest of the staff attends a training program. Then, they reverse positions.

Of course, there's the obvious other choice. Off-premises training is the least used but the most effective. This type of training is less popular because it requires sending finance managers to an F&I school. These courses can be anywhere, including distant states, and offer classes that are commonly three to five days long. Most dealerships cannot afford to be shorthanded for that long and do not take advantage of these opportunities. Nevertheless, off-premises training is the most effective because it offers a total immersion and zero distractions. I want to encourage dealer principals and general managers to send their finance managers to these type of training seminars if they want to see real improvements in product penetration and back-end profit.

Finally, there is another type of training that I rarely see. As we discussed earlier, there are Saturday morning sales meetings taking place across the country. Focus of these meetings is to train salespeople. Why not combine the sales meeting with one for the finance managers? When was the last time your finance managers had to demonstrate their product knowledge? When was the last time they had to pitch and overcome objections? Like athletes and salesmen, finance managers will improve with regular practice and training.

F&I Department Must Work Together with Service Department

F&I department is the glue that connects sales and service departments. In a successful dealership, as previously noted, all departments must work towards a common goal of improving customer experience in order to increase customer retention and profits. Remember: that sales department sells the first car to a customer, but service sells the second, third, fourth, etc.

Training remains important regardless of how you accomplish it. Service department must work together with the F&I department to know what products are being sold and how to file a claim. Regular meetings should be held between your service and parts director and your director of finance. If service advisors do not know how to file a claim or do not want to be bothered with third-party service contracts and ancillary products, your finance department will lose credibility, and it will only be harder to sell these products in the future.

It is the responsibility of the finance managers to train service advisors on the products that are being sold in F&I and how to file a claim. Finance managers should also get involved in helping service advisors get these claims approved.

Understanding Proper Workload

With all that a finance manager has to do, it's important that you don't critical aspect to job satisfaction and success: work-life balance. Below is the quote from menthalhealthamerica.net:

"While we all need a certain amount of stress to spur us on and help us perform at our best, the key to managing stress lies in that one magic word: balance. Not only is achieving a healthy work/life balance an attainable goal but workers and businesses alike see the rewards. When workers are balanced and happy, they are more productive, take fewer sick days, and are more likely to stay in their jobs."

These comments are very apropos to our industry. Dealerships are often guilty of burning out people because of the grueling schedule. That's one of the main reasons it is hard to attract competent personnel.

I am a big believer in five-day workweek. This approach allows finance managers to focus on getting customers approved, getting deals funded, and most importantly spend enough quality time with customers. Seeing an average of 3 to 3.5 customers per workday will ensure a quality interaction with customers and provide enough time to present products and build value. If your finance managers are taking more than 80 turns per month, then your dealership is burning them out while simultaneously leaving money on the table.

Keep in mind that one of the main reasons why automotive retail professionals leave the business or change jobs is spousal pressure. Finance managers must be able to spend time with their spouse and children. At present, finance managers average 50-hour workweeks nationally. That's too much. Build the schedule in a way that allows each finance manager at least one weekend off a month.

Selling Vehicle Service Contracts in Service Department

Service drive is the most natural place to offer vehicle service contracts, considering the sheer volume of cars going through the drive and the fact that many of those cars either have an expired factory warranty or one about to expire. Unfortunately, most dealerships do not capitalize on this opportunity. First and foremost, service and parts director together with the finance director should set a goal of selling x-amount of vehicle service contracts per month. Then they need to develop a plan and implement it. Below are some points to consider when developing a plan:

- Availability of a vehicle service contract that could be sold in the service drive
- Signage/ marketing materials in the service waiting area and at each service advisor's desk
- Determine pricing – for example, cost plus $1,000.
- Offer zero APR financing as vehicle service contracts are not cheap, and most consumers are not enthusiastic about the need to shell out an additional $2,000 - $3,000
- Determine whether the vehicle service contract presentation is done by a service advisor or a finance manager
- Determine the pay plan to compensate service advisors or finance managers for their sales. Remember that pay plans drive behavior. There must be proper incentives in place in order to stimulate VSC sales in the service drive.

Displaying F&I Products Online

According to the inaugural Car Buyer Journey study commissioned by Autotrader and conducted by HIS Automotive, as of 2016, more than 60 percent of the car-buying process happens online. Those figures have probably grown a lot since then. For many people, the entire car shopping process, minus the test drive, happens online as the millennial generation is placing more and more emphasis on digital communication.

Unfortunately, the automotive industry is dragging its heels when it comes to the adoption of digital, seamless and convenient online buying methods preferred by today's consumers. It's becoming increasingly essential for dealerships to offer finance information and add-ons online, unless they want customers to turn their attention elsewhere.

Currently, the majority of dealership websites are loaded with information. For example, a consumer can see the vehicles in stock, vehicles in transit, research different models, get an appraisal of their trade-in, schedule a test drive, schedule a service appointment, buy parts, but rarely can they find do what kind of F&I products are being offered. Even though every dealership's website has a Finance tab, there is very little useful information. Normally, the Finance tab only contains a credit application and lease versus finance calculator.

Most dealers continue to keep F&I a secret out of fear that full disclosure will negatively impact profitability. Instead, customers get ambushed in the showroom with a ton of new information and high-pressure sales tactics.

Internet allows consumers to research anything that they are planning to buy. If car dealers fail to display information about the F&I products that they offer, consumers will only see the negative articles telling them to stay away from these products.

It's time to bring F&I out of the shadows and into the spotlight. The F&I products and add-ons need to be presented front and center on the dealer's website. Since at least 60 percent of the car shopping process happens electronically, this is where prospective consumers can begin learning about various products before making their final decision.

A site that hides information only builds consumer frustration and distrust. Instead, embrace your F&I offerings by being upfront with consumers from the moment they open your dealership website. By having access to this information, they'll be more inclined to include the add-ons with their final purchase, as well as share the information with friends and family.

Just as importantly, today's consumers want information presented to them directly and accurately online. Dealers should showcase all available information, including features, benefits, as well as prices from the get-go. People don't want to be led in a sales circle anymore. Why? Because they can just move to another site and peruse the next dealership down the block.

In fact, they can go anywhere in the country via their computer and buy a car in a dealership thousands of miles away. Your site needs to have all the information needed for car-buying decision. It needs to be accessible and, just as importantly, monitored so a customer can receive a prompt response to questions.

This new approach can increase acceptance rates and customer satisfaction tenfold. As you know, a large chunk of customer complaints is due to the amount of time they must spend in F&I.

Menu Presentation

When it comes to presenting F&I products in the dealership menu, you need to be sure the menu is easily understood and works properly. There are great menus out there, such as MaximTrak and Darwin, that easily integrate with Reynolds & Reynolds, ADP, Dealertrack and other smaller Dealer Management Systems.

There is a misconception among many dealers and finance managers that they must use the menu in order to be compliant. There is no law on the books that mandates menu usage in car dealerships. In reality, a finance menu is a phenomenal sales tool and should be used with that understanding. A quality menu helps ensure that the finance department can do its job of obtaining the most favorable financing options for the customer as well as maximizing profitability by selling F&I products.

Menus guarantee customers are introduced to available products in a consistent manner in the briefest amount of time possible. At the same time, menus help a dealer owner determine how well the F&I manager is doing and serves as a compliance tool. To avoid overloading customers with information, menus need to be streamlined with information presented in clear, concise language. To reduce the number of options, you should consider removing products that have drawn little interest.

Menu presentation allows the finance manager to implement the 300 percent rule: 100 percent of products are presented 100 percent of the time to 100 percent of the customers. This approach is guaranteed to increase product penetration, but it doesn't mean that finance manager can sell everyone.

There are three types of customers: 20 percent are ready to buy everything and anything available; 20 percent will never buy anything; and 60 percent who need more information in order to make a buying decision. Focusing on the 60 percent will increase product penetration and profitability of the dealership.

Menu Presentation

Some finance managers start their presentation with a detailed explanation of the factory warranty and then transition into the product presentation to highlight how these products plug the holes in the factory coverage. Others go straight into the menu presentation. I personally prefer the second approach because the 20 percent of customers who are ready to buy everything do not need the information overload.

There are two schools of thought when it comes to menu layout. The first school prefers three or four columns, such as Platinum, Gold, Silver Bronze. The Platinum package has all the products under the sun; Gold has a little less, and so on.

The other school of thought is two columns: package A and package B. My personal preference is the binary layout because it reduces the number of choices and makes it easier for the customer to decide. Ultimately, there is no right or wrong answer. I have seen finance managers work miracles with both menu layouts.

Another important point is to use the declination page. Every menu on the market has a declination page; this is where the declined products are listed. High-performing finance manager use this part of the menu to their advantage, realizing it provides a second opportunity to present the features and benefits of the declined product.

They ask the customer to initial next to each product and use the following word track:

F&I: "Mr. Jones, you were quick to decline the protection. What is the main reason you prefer to self-insure?"

Customer: "What do you mean by self-insure?"

Since people do not like to self-insure anything, this is a great opportunity for the finance manager to highlight certain features and benefits of the product. In other words, this is the second opportunity to close the deal.

Customer Interview

Again, there are two schools of thought when it comes to a customer interview. The first approach is to have the finance manager do an extensive customer interview in order to understand their driving habits. The other approach is for the finance manager to meet the customer, set time expectations and build rapport. I prefer the second approach because customers understand that an extensive interview about their previous driving habits is designed to sell them stuff. An extensive interview can make the customer sales resistant, and nobody needs that.

Length of the Menu Presentation

A finance manager should try to do the entire presentation in under 5 minutes. The length of the presentation is important because finance managers must understand that the customer has been in the showroom for an extensive period. A brief and to the point presentation saves time and makes it easier for the first 20 percent of customers – the ones that will buy everything – to make a buying decision without an information overload. The other 20 percent of customers – the ones who will never buy anything – will appreciate a short presentation as well. The remaining customers might have some questions or objections. That's when the finance manager should be ready to provide an extensive explanation and/or overcome objections.

Sample Menu Presentation

Before starting the presentation, it is a good idea to have on hand documents such as title and registration paperwork, odometer disclosure statement for the trade, privacy notice, lemon law, etc., so the customer understands that this is a professional office and gets into the habit of signing.

Here is sample dialogue with a customer. After greetings:

F&I: "I want to review the sales figures with you and available protection packages."

At this point, a finance manager should review the sales price of the vehicle, cash down, taxes, applicable rebates, trade-in allowance and the base monthly payment. Remember that the base payment **does not** include any F&I products.

F&I: "Before we move forward, do all these numbers look right to you?"

Customer: "Yes, they do."

F&I: "Great. First, this is our Platinum package. It is the most popular package among our customers because it provides the ultimate piece of mind."

The following is an imaginary sales routine based on one dealership's package. You should tailor it to match your dealerships offerings.

F&I: "The Platinum package includes the vehicle service contract for 6 years, 100,000 miles. That covers everything except for basic maintenance items such as belts, hoses and oil changes.

"Next is our prepaid maintenance program for the next 3 years; it includes two oil changes per year, a tire rotation, complimentary car wash, and a ton of other benefits. You get a 30 percent discount by buying it upfront. Our service department will take great care of your vehicle.

"You might like the tire and wheel protection. We live in New York City. You know how terrible our roads are. You can hit a pothole, pop a tire, dent the rim. Before you know it, you are looking at a $1,000 bill. Our tire and wheel protection is good for the next five years. There are no mileage limitations, no deductible, no limit on claims, and, most importantly, it includes roadside assistance. As a parent, the last thing you want to do is be stuck on the side of the road while taking your kids to a soccer practice.

"You also should consider our key replacement plan. As you know, keys nowadays are very expensive – $600 to $800 on average. This plan replaces a lost or stolen key for free. Next, we have the paint and fabric protection. It will protect the paint from salt, acid rain, bird droppings and ultraviolet light. It will also protect the interior from spills, stains, rips and burns.

"If you decide to go with this package, your monthly payment will be $575 per month.

"However, you may not need all of that. Our Gold package includes everything in the platinum package except for the key replacement. So, if you lose your key, the cost to replace and reprogram the key is on you. Silver package includes everything in the Gold package except for paint and fabric protection. So, if your kids spill orange juice in the car or the paint fades because of acid rain you are stuck with the bill. Our Bronze package only includes the vehicle service contract."

Finance manager must review the payment after presenting each package.

As you can see, this presentation is short and sweet. First, you don't want to information overload the 20 percent of customers that will buy everything in the Platinum package. Second, today's customers have done the majority of their research prior to coming into the dealership and understand what F&I products are and what they are designed to do.

If the customer is on the fence or has additional questions, then the finance manager should go into the detailed explanation of the factory warranty in order to highlight the need for additional protection.

Most sophisticated dealers use electronic menus that integrate with DMS software; however, installing a menu system is not enough. It is critical to implement effective policies and procedures in order to obtain a desired outcome. Below are the most effective policies and procedures using the DMAIC process. DMAIC is the core tool used in Six Sigma projects.

- **Define the objective**: the dealer principal, general manager, or director of finance must state what the desired PVR and product penetration percentage are. Mandate menu usage.

- **Measure**: start by measuring the last 12 months of production in order to account for seasonal changes. Menu utilization reports will come in handy.
- **Analyze**: assess what products are being sold, as well as average gross profit and penetration for each product.
- **Improve**: set a desired PVR and product penetration. Train finance managers on how to effectively present the menu. Implement a pay plan that incentivizes finance managers to perform at the optimum level.
- **Control**: review and incrementally increase desired outcome on a monthly or quarterly basis.

It is essential that there is a fail-safe mechanism to make sure that finance managers are using the menu. I recommend not to bill a deal unless there is a signed menu. Another approach is to use a menu that monitors the keystrokes; this way, the dealer will know how much time the finance manager spent presenting each product. The easiest approach is to run the menu utilization report on a regular basis. It is worth mentioning again the importance of clearly spelled out policies and procedures. One of these policies should require using the menu. Regular menu training will help improve results as well. You would be surprised how many finance managers have no idea how to use an electronic menu.

Following these steps will allow the finance department to increase product penetration and gross profit while improving customer retention.

Unsold Customers Follow-Up

Unfortunately, most finance managers do not engage in any unsold follow-ups after the customer leaves their office. Often, customers decline products because their guard is up or because they spent 5 hours waiting to see the finance manager. At this point, they just want to get out of there and go home. In two weeks, when the customer is not in the dealership and there is pride of ownership, it could be a little easier to sell certain F&I products. Ignoring this fact means that these finance managers and their respective dealerships are missing out on a tremendous profit center. Again, this phenomenon occurs because unsold follow up is not in the job description of a finance managers. Most finance managers have never picked up the phone to make an outgoing follow-up call.

This strategy is guaranteed to increase product penetration. Following up should include an email and a phone call campaign. The dealership must decide whether finance managers or BDC staff will perform this important task. I prefer finance managers because they have the necessary product knowledge and sales skills.

Smooth Cancelation Process

As you know, cancelations are part of the business. Given that reality, it is essential to have a smooth cancelation process in F&I department. Lack of a smooth cancelation process will only make the problem worse.

Often, customers need to cancel F&I products they bought only to find that the cancelation process in many dealerships is not the greatest. These dealerships are guilty of giving the customer a runaround, and that's unacceptable. In most cases, if these products were properly presented and explained, there would be no need to cancel them.

There must be a written cancelation/refund process, and every finance manager must follow it. It is a good idea for the compliance officer to oversee the cancelation process. That's a good segue to the next topic.

Compliance In The F&I Department

I want to stress the importance of compliance. This is an extremely important topic, affecting the bottom line through high fines and penalties. In addition, reputational damage is hard to quantify but failure to follow the rules ultimately results in reduced lead count, floor traffic and sales. For example, Federal Trade Commission (FTC) imposes a $3,500 fine for Red Flags Rule violations and $11,000 per occurrence per day for Safeguards Rule violations. Now that the new Safeguards Rule has gone into effect in 2023, FTC can fine the dealership $46,517 per violation. Yes, you read that right – $46,517 per violation.

Another reason for having a robust compliance program is to improve an overall reputation of car dealers. Members of Congress, lobbyists and car salesmen only edged out telemarketers as having the worst reputations for honesty and ethical standards, according to a Gallup Poll. That's not how you want customers to think about your staff.

Bad reputation coupled with customer complaints is the reason why Federal and State regulators go after car dealers on a regular basis.

These investigations result in newspaper headlines that in turn contribute to the worsening reputation of car dealers. In addition, these investigations generate hundreds of thousands and even millions of dollars in fines and penalties.

For example, in 2022, the North American Automotive Services in Illinois, Florida, Pennsylvania, and Missouri agreed to a $10 million fine levied by the FTC and the State of Illinois for "a host of deceptive and unfair tactics related to hidden fees for add-ons." In another 2022 case, nine dealerships in Maryland were fined $3.38 million by the Federal Trade Commission for racial discrimination.

In both cases – and there are many more – following the rules would have saved a ton of money.

Compliance training must be the foundation of any successful dealership. Achieving a compliant F&I Department is another matter.

Every dealer should start by appointing a compliance officer and giving that person the necessary authority to enforce corporate policy and procedure as well as to conduct the required training. The compliance officer must oversee the finance department and check deal folders, listen to audio – if available – and watch the video interactions of all finance managers and customers.

Here are the recommended duties of a compliance officer.

- Lead the way in developing, implementing, enforcing and testing the dealership's compliance program to ensure organization-wide internal controls are in place
- Mentor and train dealership employees
- Assess compliance risk, correct deficiencies, identify cause of compliance exceptions and develop corrective actions
- Take responsibility for responding to any dealership or department inquiries about compliance issues.

Below are some of the key areas that a compliance officer must oversee in the finance department.

- Truth in Lending Act (TILA) and CLA disclosures
- Risk-based pricing
- Adverse action
- Safeguards Program
- Disposal Rule
- Privacy Rule
- Identity Theft Prevention Program
- Office of Foreign Asset Controls (OFAC)
- Fair Credit Compliance Program
- F&I product uniform pricing
- Menu presentation.

Good management requires vigilance. There is a way to be fair as you quietly monitor all operations around you. Unfortunately, you will generate a certain amount of fear into the process – simply by making your F&I people aware of these controls. However, the bottom line is that the dealership and its departments function in accordance with compliance rules.

Another way to insure compliance is to establish a fair credit compliance program that outlines the dealer participation rate. National Automobile Dealer Association (NADA) has done a great job creating this program. It is designed to prevent disparate impact and explains predetermined allowable deviations, including the following:

- Participation limited by a lender
- Customer has monthly payment constraint
- Competitive offer
- Dealership promotional financing campaign
- Manufacturer subvention program
- Dealership employee incentive program
- Dealership inventory reduction consideration.

These deviations must be documented and filed in a deal folder.

I strongly feel that a key area of compliance vulnerability in the F&I department is the sale of ancillary products, such as service contracts, tire and wheel protection, lease wear and tear, paint and fabric protection, and so forth. There should be a uniform pricing for all the products offered in F&I department to avoid being accused of discrimination. Like rate participation, deviations from the uniform pricing must be documented and filed in the deal folder.

Compliance efforts do not end there. Probably one of the most critical aspects is the safeguarding and disposing of consumer non-public information. The new IT requirements cover the following:

- Encryption
- Multi-factor authentication
- Systems monitoring
- Penetration testing
- Vulnerability assessments.

Compliance is not an element of owning a car dealership that can be ignored. Nationwide, auto retail profits are at the highest level in history. At the same time, in tandem, dealers are targets of investigations by state and federal agencies. Do whatever it takes to help your dealership avoid fines that can dent both your reputation and your bottom line.

To ensure a compliant F&I department, several factors must take place:

- Background checks, drug tests, and references
- Certification and ongoing training
- Effective policy and procedures and onboarding process
- F&I product and vendor assessment
- Clearly defined profit expectations for product-penetration.

Examples of Non-Compliant Practices in F&I

Each day, finance departments face major risks in order to stay in compliance. There are four major risks that I am going to discuss in greater detail. They are:

- Falsifying Credit Applications
- Power Booking Used Cars
- Payment Packing
- Jamming F&I Products.

Falsifying credit applications is a major concern. Unscrupulous finance managers reduce rent expense, increase income and years of employment in order to get larger advance from the bank. It is extremely easy to falsify Proof of Income – just go to paystubb.com. For $7, you can obtain an ADP-formatted paystub in a matter of minutes. Some financial managers have done that to obtain a more favorable approval from the bank, receiving a greater advance in order to maximize the profit.

Another area of concern is power booking used cars, which means that finance managers exaggerate the value of used cars by telling the bank that the car has options – but really doesn't – such as leather interior and sunroof, again to get a larger bank advance.

In addition, financial managers have drawn fines for payment packing and jamming F&I products. Payment packing – the deceptive act of presenting inflated monthly car loan payments to customers during negotiations – follows when a rogue finance manager obtains loan approval from a bank. Jamming F&I products refers to slipping products into these inflated car payments without customers' knowledge or consent.

This offense is high on the agenda of state and federal law enforcement agencies. The New York Attorney General has gone after numerous car dealers in the last three years and collected millions of dollars in fines and penalties. Recently a Nissan dealership in New York was fined $298,000 and Hyundai dealership in New Jersey was fined $136,000 for these exact practices.

The end results of these illegal practices are high payments, cancelations, customer complaints, reputational damage and repossessions.

As you know, the F&I is an extremely important department. If not properly run, the department can cause tremendous losses – financial and reputational – through noncompliant and unethical practices. Today's progressive dealership employs a compliance officer and has strong internal controls.

PART 2

Reinsurance of F&I Products

Of course, many dealers use outside businesses to insure various products. This section is going to look at the administration fees charged by a third-party administrator to administer an F&I product contract.

As discussed before, there are costs associated with developing an administrator contract and getting it approved by each state, including printing, marketing and, most importantly, method of adjudicating any claim. That sounds straightforward but it is not. Third-party administrators have their own definition of the administration fee.

I have often met with car dealers who are considering some form of participation structure. In most cases, the one question that they usually ask is: how much is the administration fee? This obsession with the dollar amount doesn't help these dealers. All they hear is a number. For example, $190 per vehicle service contract sounds better than $205. On face value I would agree unless you realize that the $190 may not be an all-inclusive fee. If you don't know whether or not there are additional fees, it is impossible to determine which fee will provide the best administration for the price.

Administration Fee and Other Fees

There are a variety of fees that may be hidden in a third-party administrator's bid.

Ceding Fee

Imagine going to the bank to deposit a $1,000 into your account. The teller gives you a receipt showing a $900 balance. You immediately wonder where the missing $100 went. If you discovered that the bank without your knowledge charged you $100 to make the deposit, you are likely to find another bank without that fee, and quickly.

Nevertheless, that's what third-party administrators may do. They may slip in a ceding fee, which is the percentage of the premium dollars that the third-party administrator charges to deposit the funds into your reinsurance company. I have seen ceding fees as high as 15 percent of the premium amount. That's worse than the imaginary bank's 10 percent deposit fee.

Suppose that you are paying an admin fee of $190, but there is also a 10 percent ceding fee. For every $1,000 dollars in premium you will pay $100 in ceding fees. As a result, your real admin fee is $290, not the $190 you think you are supposed to pay. Just imagine how much money you could be wasting in ceding fees. The moral of the story is that the ceding fee is an awesome profit center for the third-party administrator that takes a huge bite of your profits.

Loss Adjustment Fee

According to Investopedia: "A loss adjustment expense is a cost insurance companies shoulder to investigate and settle insurance claims."

Briefly put, loss adjusters investigate insurance claims in various fields covered by insurance companies. They are responsible for figuring out how much damage or loss the insurance policy covers and then advising the insurer based on that coverage.

In case of any type of reinsurance, a Loss Adjustment Fee refers to the investigation of a mechanical breakdown claim for a vehicle service contract. It could also refer to the investigation of claims regarding tires and wheels, key replacement, combo products, etc.

Loss Adjustment Fee is the percentage of the claim amount that the third-party administrator charges to adjudicate claims. There are third-party administrators that charge as much as 10 percent. For example, a customer has a water pump claim that is covered by the vehicle service contract. The claim amount paid is $2,400. Third-party administrator would deduct 10 percent or $240 from the reinsurance company reserves to offset the loss adjustment fee.

Let's go back to the earlier example of $190 versus the $205 admin fee. If the $205 admin fee is all in – meaning, there is no extra charge for ceding and/or loss adjustment fee – then it is a better deal than the $190 admin fee because ceding and loss adjustment fees will be tacked on.

Premium Tax

Premium tax is a state-specific tax. As the name implies, the premium amount is what gets taxed. Most third-party administrators charge a flat 2.5 percent regardless of the state the dealer does business in; however, there are some third-party administrators that charge a state-specific premium tax. It is important to know that not all states have a premium tax. As a result, you should check on each state in which your dealership operates to ensure this is a necessary expense. Keep in mind that some third-party administrators include the premium tax in the admin fee while others charge separately for it.

Cancelation Fees

We all know what cancelation fees are. When the customer decides to cancel a vehicle service contract or any other F&I product, a third-party administrator charges a fee that normally ranges from $50 to $75. This is another profit center for third-party administrators in the reinsurance or retro environment. Keep in mind that with a Dealer Owned Warranty Company (DOWC), all cancellation fees go back to the DOWC and not to a third-party administrator.

Custodial Fees for Trust Accounts

As discussed before, money managers invest premium dollars by a money manager regardless of whether a dealer forms a Controlled Foreign Corporation (CFC), a Non-Controlled Foreign Corporation (NCFC) or DOWC. Money managers do not do that out of the goodness of their heart. They charge a fee. Fees assessed by the investment manager who oversees the brokerage account are known as custodial costs for trust accounts. Average fees are approximately 1 percent of funds under management.

Segregated Cell Fee

This is a fee that a third-party administrator charges for segregating GAP from other F&I products. This prevents comingling of premiums. In turn, this means that if the Gap insurance portfolio goes upside down, the contractual liability insurance policy (CLIP) kicks in. If products are not segregated, then the premium dollars generated by VSC, and ancillary product sales will initially cover the Gap insurance losses.

Run-Off Fee

Dealers who decides to stop writing into their reinsurance company commonly face a run-off fee. Run-off fee is the percentage of the unearned premium. As unearned premium goes down, so does the run-off fee. In most cases, a dealer makes a decision to stop writing because he finds a better deal with another third-party administrator.

Annual Fee

Annual fees are a part of life of a Controlled Foreign Corporation (CFC) and Non-Controlled Foreign Corporation (NCFC). On average, CFC dealers are charged between $3,500 and $5,000 per year for maintenance that covers domicile, books and records. NCFC dealers are paying an average of $25,000 per year. DOWC, on the other hand, doesn't have annual maintenance fees. The only fee that

DOWC will incur on the annual basis covers the preparation of tax returns.

Tax Returns Fee

Dealers with a Controlled Foreign Corporation must file a federal tax return every year. Those who have started a Dealer Owned Warranty Company must file both federal and state returns every year. Dealers who have a Non-Controlled Foreign Corporation do not need to file a return of any kind. The fee for preparing tax returns – the average is $3,000 per year – is in addition to the annual fee.

All-In Administration Fee

Now that you understand that there are many additional fees, you should really understand how much is the "all-in" admin fee that you are paying. The key takeaway here is that admin fee alone should never be the focus of negotiations with an agent or a third-party administrator. Instead, you must focus on the "all-in" admin fee to see what your true costs will be.

Once you do that, you will recognize, as I have emphasized, that a DOWC will give you ultimate transparency and control.

Different Types of Participation Programs

Reinsurance, which you know as any type of a vehicle service contract or an "extended warranty," can have a real impact on your bottom line. There are several types of participation programs available:

- No participation or walkaway
- Retro
- Reinsurance
- Dealer Owned Warranty Company.

Before we get into nitty gritty of different participation programs, let's talk about car racing. I'm not actually getting offtrack. You will soon see the connection.

Imagine that there is a car race where all types of cars are allowed to compete. Can you finish a race in a regular production car like a Toyota Corolla? Absolutely. But we both know that you won't win the race. If you want to improve your results, you need to upgrade your car – get something faster, something with more horsepower like a Ford Mustang. Most likely you would finish in top five but still wouldn't win the race. If you are serious about getting on the podium with other great racers, you need to start thinking about a Ferrari or a Lamborghini, a car with real speed and awesome cornering. Finally, to finish first, you would need a Formula 1 car. It offers incredible acceleration, braking, cornering, and overall amazing handling.

This book is supposed to be about F&I, so why are we talking about car racing? Because selling F&I products and choosing the right participation structure will be the difference between simply finishing and actually winning the race to success for a dealership.

The last thing we need to discuss before we get into different types of participation structures is the composition of each F&I product. For example, if the cost of the vehicle service contract is $1,000, how is this price chosen? The answer is simple – around $800 is the premium. The premium is there to pay future claims.

Every third-party administrator or an insurance company has an actuarial department whose job is to compile and analyze statistics to calculate insurance risks and premiums. In the United States, we have data going back decades that pertains to reliability of different types of cars and trucks. This historical data allows the actuarial department to figure out premiums for both new and used cars.

If the actuarial department does a good job, then, by the time the contract expires, there will be underwriting profit. Underwriting profit equals premium minus claims paid. In addition to underwriting profit, third-party administrator or insurance company enjoys investment income. Remember that premium dollars are not sitting idly in the bank; they are being actively invested.

The other $200 of the premium is the cost associated with administering this vehicle service contract. Those costs include developing the contract, getting it approved by each state to be sold, printing, marketing, and, most importantly, adjudicating the claim.

As you can see, there are numerous costs associated with each F&I product. Third-party administrators have many people on the payroll –claims adjusters, attorneys, graphic designers, salespeople, etc. In my opinion, claim adjudication is key and separates good and bad third-party administrators. When a vehicle breaks down, either the customer or the service advisor must call the administrator to start the claim. Claims adjusters must determine if this is a covered repair, so they need to understand the coverage and have technical knowledge. Good adjusters are usually ASE certified and have worked as technicians or service managers. ASE certification is obtained from the National Institute of Automotive Service Excellence.

If this is a covered repair, claims adjuster must request all the necessary support documents, such as copy of the repair order, receipts, etc. Finally, the payment must be processed. Depending on the type of the contract and the preference of the repair facility, payment can be made in several ways. Third-party administrator can pay with a virtual credit card or mail the check. Also, if this happens to be a reimbursement policy, then the customer pays the service facility and later gets reimbursed by check.

Walkaway

Let's start with the first type of participation structure – walkaway. Walkaway simply means that a dealership sells different types of F&I products and makes money by marking up these products. For example, if the cost of the vehicle service contract is $1,000, and a finance manager sells it for $2,500, then your dealership is sitting pretty with a $1,500 gross profit. That profit is taxable income. Once the sale is made, it doesn't really matter to the selling dealer if the premium dollars are going to exceed the claims or vice versa. In other words, the dealer is not participating in the underwriting and investment income. This is a very straightforward approach: both independents and new car stores sell walkaway products. These stores for variety of reasons – mostly due to failure to understand other types of participation structures – just want to finish the race and, in the process, end up leaving a ton of money on the table.

Retro

Retro allows the dealership to participate in the underwriting and/or investment income, depending on the program. A dealer is paid a portion of underwriting/investment profit as the business earns out. The payments are made directly to the dealership, and the dealer assumes no risk. The payment to the dealership is taxable income. Retro creates an additional profit center for the dealer. The portion of the profit that will be split with the dealership will be outlined in the agreement.

The ratio can be 100 percent. In this situation, the insurer returns the entire underwriting profit to the dealership while keeping its administrative charge and investment income. The insurer might only split a portion of the profit with smaller dealerships. There are high-volume dealers that choose to be in a retro because they don't want to deal with formations of foreign companies and/or future tax consequences. This is the proverbial Ford Mustang: you are going fast but not fast enough to finish in top five or win the race.

Admin Obligor versus Dealer Obligor

We briefly discussed this subject in the beginning of the book. This topic is important, so it is worth it to review it in detail. In simple terms, admin obligor means that the third-party administrator is on the hook to pay the claims. Dealer obligor means the dealer is responsible.

There are several reasons why a dealer may set up a reinsurance company, such as wealth building via underwriting and investment profits as well as through preferential taxation. A properly set up reinsurance company is not taxed on the underwriting profits and only pays qualified dividend tax rate on the investment profit. Also, a properly set up reinsurance company has products that are admin obligor.

Keep in mind, that there are third-party administrators that offer dealer obligor programs. Why would a dealer want to sign up for a dealer obligor program? The answer is simple – cash flow. In the dealer obligor program, dealer remits an administration fee to the third-party administrator while all the reserves stay in the dealership. These reserves become part of the profit and loss statement where they are subject to ordinary income tax treatment. So, right off the bat, a dealer that participates in the dealer obligor program gives up a big chunk of profits in taxes.

Also, many dealers are guilty of using the reserves to acquire inventory, to cover floor plan expenses or to plug other financial holes. Moreover, many dealers fail to set aside the proper dollar amount to pay future claims. This requires stellar financial discipline. Ultimately, improper management of reserves means that dealers are in a never-ending rat race. They must continue selling F&I products to cover claims that are only increasing the longer they are in the program. If there are not enough reserves to pay the claims, the claims will be made against the dealership. If the dealership has no money, the claims will be made against the dealer personally.

The last point on the dealer obligor programs is critical for you to understand. All the future claims are the liabilities sitting on your profit and loss statement. One day, if the dealer decides to sell the dealership, the value of future claims – liabilities – could be greater than the value of the blue sky. My advice is to think long and hard before signing up for a dealer obligor program.

Reinsurance

Due to a lack of knowledge about the advantages or apprehension over the risks, many dealers choose not to establish their own reinsurance companies. My goal is to demystify reinsurance, so car dealers can increase profits and build generational wealth.

The formation of a dealer's own reinsurance company often results in an increase in a dealership's profitability. In many cases, customers are required to return to the selling dealer to do the repairs. This approach increases profits in both parts and service. Then, as the dealers see premium dollars accumulating, they become more cognizant of increasing product penetration through the F&I department.

Most importantly, the dealer retains 100 percent of underwriting and investment profits. On the flipside, the dealer participates in the losses as well.

There are two types of automotive reinsurance companies, both of which have been mentioned previously – Controlled Foreign Corporation (CFC) and Non-Controlled Foreign Corporation (NCFC).

Controlled Foreign Corporation (CFC)

Controlled Foreign Corporation (CFC) is 100 percent owned by the dealer and in majority of cases domiciled in Turks and Caicos. Recently, the Delaware Tribe of Indians has become a popular domicile as well. Dealers have traditionally domiciled their reinsurance companies in foreign countries for various reasons, including lower costs and easier regulatory requirements. For example, Turks and Caicos requires minimum initial capital to start. On average, formation cost of a CFC is around $5,000. Once the CFC is formed, it makes a 953(d) election. A foreign insurance company that makes a 953(d) election is treated as a domestic corporation. It is not taxed as a foreign corporation. Therefore, premiums paid by Americans to a foreign insurance company, which has made a 953(d) election, are not subject to the Federal Excise Tax. This is a great reason for choosing a 953(d) election. It means that 100 percent of the premiums received by the foreign insurance company will be available to pay claims filed by clients of the insurance company.

Next step is the 831(b) election under the Internal Revenue Code. Insurance companies who have elected for the IRC § 831(b) small insurance company tax regime may write up to $2,650,000 in 2023 and qualify for the exclusion of underwriting income from taxable income. Yes, you read it right – underwriting profits are not taxed. In other words, only investment income is subject to income tax. We are driving a Ferrari now.

Where is the money being held? I am sure that a lot of dealers would be uncomfortable with keeping their money offshore. The good news is that since the CFC is treated as a domestic corporation, it can open a bank account in the United States.

The reason for the increasing popularity of the Delaware Indian Tribe domicile is because it eliminates the need for the 953(d) election and makes it easier to open a bank account in the United States.

Now that you have formed your insurance company domiciled in Turks and Caicos with a bank account in the United States, you are ready to start doing business. But let's be honest here – car dealers may know how to run a car dealership, how to sell cars, parts, and provide service, but they do not know how to run an insurance company. This is where the expertise of the third-party administrators come in handy. This is also where the concept of reinsurance comes into play.

Reinsurance, or insurance for insurers, transfers risk to another company to reduce the likelihood of large payouts for a claim. Remember the composition of the vehicle service contract or any other F&I product? It consists of two parts – premium and administration fee. Part of the administration fee is the Contractual Liability Insurance Policy (CLIP), which helps cover claims related to contract issues. There is a CLIP on every contract sold by the finance department. For example, suppose there is $500,000 in premiums in the dealer owned reinsurance company. These premium dollars are from the sale of both vehicle service contracts and ancillary products. As claims come in, they are paid from the collected premium. Hypothetically, once the claims reach $500,001 and there is no more money to pay the claims, a CLIP will kick in to pay the claims.

As the dealership keeps selling F&I products, and premium dollars keep coming into the reinsurance company, several things are happening at the same time. First, the premium dollars are being invested. Keep in mind that these investments are very conservative because high-risk investments might go belly up, leaving insufficient funds to pay future claims. Normally, these investments guidelines are set by the third-party administrators (TPA). Most TPAs offer these options: 80/20 or 90/10 – either 10 percent or 20 percent is allocated towards stocks while 80 percent or 90 percent is allocated towards fixed income.

In addition, as the contracts earn out, the earned premium is moved to another account, called a B account, which can be invested in whatever manner the dealer wants. For example, if the dealer wants to invest 100 percent of the money in the B account in crypto or a particular stock, no one will stop him. Keep in mind that the B account can be opened in the bank of the dealer's choice. It doesn't need to be in the same bank where the Trust account is. To avoid tax ramifications, B account must be opened in the name and tax ID of the reinsurance company.

Annual Premium Limit

As discussed above, as of 2023, an insurance company that takes an 831(b) election can write up to $2,650,000 in annual premium. This is an important point to understand: the $2,650,000 limit resets to zero every year.

However, if you exceed this limit, there are serious penalties. If the 831(b) election is misused, the IRS may tax the dealership on its premium income in addition to denying the operating firm that paid the premiums a deduction for its expenses. If the IRS determines the structure to be abusive, significant fines and interest may also be imposed. Therefore, care must be used to avoid forming an 831(b) Captive solely for tax savings; meaningful business and non-tax economic purpose must be objectives of the design and management decisions. Third-party administrators must monitor on the regular basis the amount of premium written in order to reduce IRS scrutiny.

Ownership of 831(b) Captive

Another important point to keep in mind is that you can own 100 percent of a company that has made an 831(b) election. If you choose to open a second reinsurance company, then you can only own 50 percent of shares. The other 50 percent cannot be owned by a spouse, but can be controlled by a business partner, trust or children over 21 years of age. Dealers can further improve the benefits of their estate plan by avoiding the inheritance tax if the 831(b) captive is controlled by trusts or adult children.

Another option is to reward key employees with shares in the reinsurance company. For example, if you wants to retain a talented general manager or director of finance, you could form a reinsurance company together with these key employees. This is what you might call "golden handcuffs." General manager or the finance director could only access the profits of the reinsurance company once it is in runoff or in five years, so they can't leave. Keep in mind that the "golden handcuffs" are much easier to implement with DOWC structure.

Abuses of 831(b) Captives

The easiest and most common type of abuse is the exaggerated premiums. For example, a $3,000 premium for a 3 year/48,000-mile vehicle service contract for a Toyota Corolla is excessive and will be scrutinized by IRS. In other words, it will be treated as a tax avoidance scheme as opposed to a legitimate premium payment to an insurance company.

Another type of abuse involves not meeting the new risk diversification requirement, which states that no one policyholder may be responsible for more than 20 percent of the net or direct written premiums, whichever is higher. Any policyholders who are related or belong to the same regulated group are treated as a single policyholder for the purpose of evaluating whether the 20 percent threshold has been reached.

Taking Profits

Since the reinsurance company is a profit center, there will be a time when these profits will need to be used to grow the business or to buy out a partner. Profits can be taken as a Qualified Dividend, which, as defined by the United States Internal Revenue Code, are ordinary dividends that meet specific criteria to be taxed at the lower long-term capital gains tax rate rather than at higher tax rate reserved for an individual's ordinary income.

Another option is to borrow from the reinsurance company. If the dealer takes a loan, then there are no taxes; however, the dealer must pay the loan back with interest like any other loan. The smart approach is to take an interest-only loan. Here is a fun fact: most third-party administrators allow dealers to borrow not just the earned premium but also a portion of the unearned premium. Once the dealer has been writing for several years, third-party administrators can accurately determine a loss ratio per product line as well as the overall loss ratio of the portfolio. Essentially, a TPA can calculate the present value of future claims.

An insurance company's actuarial present value is the amount of money it projects needing in order to pay for the promised benefits. This figure is based on the payments received from the insured, the interest rate, and the probable time and frequency at which the company will have to provide the promised benefits. For example, if the average loss ratio is 50 percent, then the TPA will let the dealer borrow up to 40 percent of unearned reserves. The remaining 10 percent serves as a buffer just in case there is a spike in claims.

Another scenario is the run-off, which occurs when the last written contract is earned. In this case the dealer must take a dividend distribution. This is the definition of a forced distribution.

I hope you are beginning to see how powerful this Ferrari is. Let's summarize the benefits so far:

- Premium paid by the dealership to the reinsurance company is deductible against ordinary income on the dealership's books.
- Underwriting profit is not subject to income tax.
- Investment profit is taxed at capital gains tax rate.
- Dealer can borrow earned and portions of unearned premium without creating a taxable event.
- Formed offshore not for tax reasons but because of lower capital requirements and less burdensome regulation.

Non-Controlled Foreign Corporations (NCFC)

According to GPW and Associates, an ultimate authority on reinsurance formation:

"An NCFC reinsurance program is a non-controlled foreign corporation domiciled in an offshore country that is owned by at least 11 unaffiliated U.S. participating shareholders or actual foreign owners. The company is typically controlled by the administrator and/or insurance company whose products are reinsured into the NCFC. The participating shareholders own a series of participating stock but do not individually direct the operations of the company or any of the investments."

Dealer doesn't form a new NCFC the way he does CFC. Instead, the dealer buys non-voting stock in an existing NCFC.

When would a dealer choose a NCFC instead of a CFC? The short answer is that a NCFC has no premium dollar limit. For example, if your dealership or auto group is going to write more than $2,650,000 in a calendar year – the premium dollar limit in a CFC – then NCFC structure must be considered. Another reason is the returns. NCFC returns historically have been higher compared with CFC and DOWC because NCFC doesn't pay taxes on either investment or underwriting profit. However, these higher returns could be wiped out by the sky-high formation and maintenance fees.

Surprisingly, there are many smaller dealers that prefer to be in a NCFC. Remember that the actual NCFC is controlled by the third-party administrator or the insurance company. Oftentimes, TPA would take a cell and park 10 dealers in one cell. That means that the formation cost is split 10 ways.

There is big difference between a CFC and a NCFC when it comes to taxation. Remember that a CFC is taxed on the investment income only, but not taxed on the underwriting profit. A NCFC is not taxed on both investment and underwriting profits. That's right – zero tax on both types of profits. But keep in mind that when the dealer decides to bring back the money to this country – "repatriate" – the USA charges a 1 percent excise tax on the funds.

Now let's talk about the difference between Controlled and Non-Controlled. First, a NCFC is truly offshore; meaning the bank account is offshore. Because a NCFC avoids current taxation on underwriting profit and investment income, shareholders make no special elections. Profits sit offshore. Second, a car dealer who owns a CFC can take a distribution or a dividend whenever he or she needs the money. A NCFC doesn't work like that. If the dealer needs to take a distribution, it must be approved by the board of directors that meets twice a year. Normally, board members are other car dealers in the NCFC. The same process applies to dealer loans.

Next, in the CFC, a dealer has some decision-making authority when it comes to the investment. At the very minimum, a dealer can choose between an 80/20 or 90/10 portfolio. Also, 100 percent of funds in the B account in the CFC can be invested at the dealer's discretion. In the NCFC, the largest dealers make all investment decisions. As a result, smaller dealerships may be partners, but have little say.

Another difference between a CFC and a NCFC is how the funds are kept. Let's assume a dealer owns a single rooftop or a small auto group. All the premium dollars sent to the insurance company come from the stores that the dealer owns. If there are losses coming from a particular product or location, reserves can be adjusted upwards relatively quickly. Again, the dealer is in control. In the NCFC, funds from all the dealerships are comingled. There could be losses in the portfolio of dealerships that the dealer has no connection to, but the overall losses will negatively impact all NCFC participants.

One more difference between a CFC and a NCFC is where they are domiciled. As discussed before, majority of Controlled Foreign Corporations are domiciled in the Turks and Caicos or the Delaware Indian Tribes. Non-Controlled Foreign Corporations can be domiciled all over the world, including, for example, the Bahamas, Bermuda, Seychelles and the United Kingdom.

Formation and maintenance costs also vary greatly. As discussed, a CFC formation is around $5,000 along with an annual charge for tax returns and maintenance fees. In a NCFC, the annual maintenance fees are around $25,000. A smaller dealer may only have to pay $2,500 to be a part of the cell in the NCFC but has no control of anything that happens in terms of investment, loans, etc.

Before the recently approved Tax Cuts and Jobs Act (TCJA), major dealers and groups could reinsure F&I products using a NCFC structure, deferring income taxation until it was repatriated – taken as a dividend or liquidated distribution from the NCFC.

Profits that were repatriated after liquidation were normally taxed at 23.8 percent as capital gains. Such a result is comparable to a CFC without the $2.3 million yearly premium cap, but with the small insurance business election.

As a result, large dealer groups have found this structure appealing, but they might have trouble locating a similar structure in the future. The tax legislation has been altered in numerous ways by the TCJA to restrict this choice for most dealers. Although though some of these structures might still be accessible following the TCJA, their use is significantly more constrained by the new regulations. In addition, taxation may have changed. I encourage dealers that are currently in a NCFC structure to consider a Dealer Owned Warranty Company (DOWC) because of these concerns about a CFC or a NCFC:

- No limit when it comes to premium writing
- As a part owner, dealer has no decision-making authority over investment or distribution timing
- Potential risk sharing with other dealers in the NCFC
- Truly offshore –domicile and bank account
- Unclear future due to TCJA.

Dealer Owned Warranty Company (DOWC)

In the recent years, the popularity of Dealer Owned Warranty Company has increased. Many dealers might be under impression that DOWC is a new and shiny object. Actually, DOWC has been on the market for more than 40 years. Unfortunately, third-party administrators often misunderstand this particular participation structure. As a result, many dealers are missing a great opportunity for generational wealth-building. The goal of this section is to demystify the Dealer Owned Warranty Company.

What is a Dealer Owned Warranty Company?

The purpose of the DOWC is to provide vehicle service contracts and ancillary products to the dealership/auto group that the dealer owns.

Unlike CFC and NCFC, a DOWC is a domestic C-corporation domiciled onshore, usually in the state where the dealership is located. Since DOWC is a domestic C-corporation, the cost of formation is significantly lower. Normally, C-corporation formation costs a few hundred dollars compared to more than thousands of dollars for a CFC and/or a NCFS. Right there, you have significant savings. Being domestically incorporated also makes it far easier to open the necessary bank accounts.

According to GPW and Associates:

"The company is not regulated as an insurance company but is treated as an insurance company for federal income tax purposes. The DOWC is owned by a dealer or dealer group and is administered by a third-party provider. The DOWC usually purchases an excess of loss insurance policy from a third-party insurance company to insure its performance under the obligations the DOWC issues."

First, the dealer forms a C-corporation to underwrite vehicle service contracts and ancillary products. Second, the dealer no longer needs a third-party administrator to hold the reserves. Reserves are held in the investment account with the money manager that the dealer can choose. When it comes to investing, there is a big difference between DOWC and a CFC. Remember that in the CFC, the dealer can invest no more than 20 percent in equities. DOWC rules allows up to 40 percent to be invested in equities. In addition, the B account in the CFC model is called an investment account in the DOWC. The investment account is not subject to 60/40 split and could be invested even more aggressively if the dealer chooses or if the investment horizon allows.

Third-party administrator notifies the money manager quarterly how much money – earned premium – can be transferred into the investment account. This is one of the major reasons why returns in a DOWC are historically higher than in a CFC.

Third, DOWC and an insurance company are the only two domestic entities that could write a vehicle service contract and receive a beneficial tax treatment called tax deferral, which allows the dealer to build generational wealth. Basically, dealers are enjoying the same tax law as the insurance companies without having to spend millions of dollars on initial capital as well as on administration and compliance. In other words, dealer's DOWC keeps the underwriting and investment profits. Most importantly, the company's lack of taxable income is caused by a number of expenses, including administration and acquisition costs for the current tax year and net operating losses that are carried forward.

Private Labeling and Customizing F&I Products

Another great advantage of the DOWC structure is the ability to white label F&I products. For example, AutoNation started selling self-branded service contracts in 50 Texas dealerships in May 2015. By the end of that year, all F&I products were sold under the AutoNation name.

"By extending the brand AutoNation to mean something, you have to take it to be more than just a name on the store," the CEO of AutoNation said. "Every time I sell an AutoNation product that delights a customer, like a service contract, it further binds customers to us in another new way, rather than handing them off to a warranty company."

In addition, private-labeled products increase service retention. Many AutoNation customers are going back to AutoNation service departments with AutoNation vehicle service contracts, far exceeding those with third-party contracts.

In a vast majority of CFC and NCFC structures, dealers sell off-the shelf F&I products. A DOWC is different – it allows the dealer to create custom coverages, rates, and marketing materials. Custom coverages/terms can give a dealer a competitive edge.

Loan Management Account

Money manager sets up three accounts for a DOWC. First, is the operating account. This is not a fee-based account designed to pay claims at outside repair facilities, admin fees due to the third-party administrator, over remits, etc. An operating account is nothing more than a checking account for the DOWC. Normal and ordinary expenses are paid from it on a monthly basis. The balance should be about two to three months of normal expenses. Second, there is the pledged account. This is a fee-based account that contains premium dollars. Money in this account is invested according to the 60/40 split: 60 percent in fixed income; 40 percent in equities. Finally, there is an investment account where the earned premium is located. This is a fee-based account like a B-account in the CFC.

What I really like about the DOWC set up is that you can use your DOWC portfolio as collateral and open a credit line in order to fund future acquisitions, showroom improvements, etc. You don't have to liquidate your portfolio. For example, you might have a 5 percent interest on your credit line, but your portfolio could be returning 7 percent. That math is a no-brainer.

Keep in mind that in a DOWC, you can borrow against the earned premium as well as up to 50 percent of unearned premium. That's huge if the dealer is in the acquisition mode.

DOWC Admin Fee

The real reason a dealer opens a DOWC is to have ultimate control and transparency. There are many hidden fees in the traditional reinsurance company. The third-party administrator that I work with has a simple all-in admin fee, eliminating the common hidden costs:

- No ceding fee
- No loss adjustment fee
- No segregated cell fee
- No premium taxes
- No excise tax
- No runoff fee
- No maintenance fee.

When the dealer doesn't have to pay any of these fees, it is easy to see why DOWC is a more profitable and the Ferrari of participation structures. Dealers that want to win the generational wealth building race must do it via a DOWC structure.

To summarize, a DOWC has these advantages:

- Customization and private labelling of F&I products
- Domiciled in the United States
- Transparent all-in admin fees
- Aggressive investment guidelines
- Insurance company taxation
- Lower loss ratios due to lower expenses compared to CFC
- Cancelation fees payable to the DOWC, not to the TPA.

Warehousing

Once the dealer principal makes the decision to form a CFC/NCFC or DOWC, a third-party administrator will warehouse all the premiums written while the formation process is taking place. It could take up to six months to complete the formation process; therefore, most warehouse agreements are up to one year. Once the formation is completed, all the funds are transferred from the warehouse account to the trust account. Dealers should make sure that the third-party administrators are paying interest on the funds that are being warehoused.

Reinsurance Review

There has never been a better time for a reinsurance review than now. Studies show that more than 55 percent of all dealers in the U.S. are now participating in reinsurance and 20 percent are participating in retro participation programs.

I am amazed at how many dealers are not reinsuring their service contract business as well as some of their ancillary products.

Reinsurance is an excellent source of income as well as a great tax strategy.

I am also surprised at how many dealers participate in some form of reinsurance without really understanding or knowing what they are paying for. It is a good idea for car dealers to have a reinsurance review on a regular basis. You now know that there could be many hidden fees besides the admin fee. Many times, a deep dive into the existing reinsurance structure would uncover the "all-in" admin fee of $400 - $500 per vehicle service contract.

Selling Reinsurance/Dealer Owned Warranty Company

There comes a time when a dealer might want to retire, sell the business, and ride into the sunset. Selling the dealership is a relatively straightforward process. Market dictates how many multiples each franchise is worth plus the value of real estate. When it comes to selling the reinsurance company/dealer owned warranty company, you have options.

First, you can sell it together with the dealership. Second option is called recapture, which occurs when you sell your participation structure back to the third-party administrator. Usually, this type of a sale involves an up to a 50 percent haircut. In other words, the price of the company is 50 percent of the unearned premium. All the earned premium belongs to the dealer and must be taken as a forced distribution. The third option is for the dealer to keep the reinsurance/dealer owned warranty company until the very last contract is earned out.

PART 3

Word Tracks That Work

There are two schools of thought when it comes to word tracks, which are defined as any statements used to address the questions and concerns of customers. There are trainers that wholeheartedly believe in word tracks while others think that word tracks are robotic. I belong to the first category. To me, word tracks make a huge a difference between an average and an excellent finance manager. A capable finance manager has multiple word tracks in his repertoire: one for the menu presentation; one for overcoming objections, one for building value in each product, etc.

They are effective because finance managers should have prepared a stellar presentation in order to be effective at their job. On top of that, customers' objections are invariably the same. If you know what the objections are ahead of time, then shame on you for not having rebuttals on the tip of your tongue.

Moreover, word tracks committed to memory are no different from so-called muscle memory in professional athletes who rely on repetition when it comes to sports, making them more effective on the field. I urge finance managers to find or create word tracks that make sense and use them on every delivery. Remember to allow for personalization, as building rapport and trust with customers while understanding their concerns and pain points plays a key role in growing sales. After all, no one wants to buy from salespeople who sound like they are reading the same script to every customer who walks in their office.

In addition, every finance manager should have an evidence manual binder, which contains sample repair orders for most common breakdowns such as air conditioning, electrical issues, etc. There also should be total loss letters and insurance settlement letters; these letters will come in handy when the finance manager introduces Gap insurance. Finally, there should be copies of repair orders showing the cost of key replacement and wheel repair/replacement.

People process information differently and there is evidence that 65 percent of the general population are visual learners. That is why the idiom "seeing is believing" makes perfect sense. Evidence manual is an awesome tool that builds the case for F&I products and overcomes customer objections. Unfortunately, many finance managers do not take advantage of this simple approach.

Overcoming Objections

Vehicle Service Contract Word Tracks

As mentioned before, the vehicle service contract is the ultimate profit generator in finance department. Keep in mind that word track is the finishing touch, the cherry on top. The real strength of finance managers comes from superior product knowledge of each product that they sell. Below are just a few examples of effective word tracks.

Variable versus Fixed Payment

Customer: "I don't think extended warranty is worth it."

F&I: "No problem. Please understand that your base monthly payment is not all inclusive. Here is what I mean – your base monthly payment of $550 is not a guarantee of the maximum out of pocket that you will pay in case of an unforeseen repair. For example, an average repair in our service department is $600. If you had to cover this type of a repair, your monthly payment during that month would be $1,150 instead of $550. As you can see, the maximum payment is really variable. On the other hand, purchasing a vehicle service contract is the guarantee that your payment will be fixed no matter how large the repair bill. Remember, this service contract covers everything except for the maintenance items and has a zero deductible. I am sure that you don't like surprises that could hurt your financially. Paying additional $40 per month for a vehicle service contract will provide you with a true fixed payment for repairs. Does that make sense to you?"

Reliable Car

Customer: "I am buying a Toyota Camry; it is one of the most reliable cars on the market."

F&I: "That's exactly right. You made the right choice buying this car. But let me ask you this, if you drove this Camry for 7 years or 100,000 miles and only spent one day in our service department, would you agree that you've purchased a great car?"

Customer: "Absolutely!"

F&I: "I'd like to show you something. Currently our labor rate is $150 per hour. For each dollar in labor, there is a dollar in parts sales. So you are looking at $300 per hour between labor and parts. If the repair takes 8 hours, then the final bill would be $2,400. The price of the vehicle service contract is only $1,800. Right off the bat, you are saving $600, plus you get all the additional benefits – towing, rental, and ability to use any licensed service facility in the country. Not to mention the inflation protection since no one knows what the labor rates are going to be like in the future. Remember, this service contract covers everything except for the maintenance items and has a zero deductible. Would you agree that having your car in the shop just for one day is expensive?"

Customer: "Yes."

F&I: "With that in mind, doesn't it make sense for you to take advantage of the vehicle service contract and enjoy a piece of mind?"

Reliable Car #2

Customer: "This is my third Honda Accord. There isn't a more reliable car out there."

F&I: "I agree with you wholeheartedly. But let me ask you this, would you buy this car without a factory warranty?"

Customer: "Of course not."

F&I: "When do you think would be the greatest probability of a breakdown – in the first three years or during the three years after that? If you wouldn't buy this car without the warranty during the first three years, why wouldn't you buy a vehicle service contract that covers the next three years?"

Reliable Car #3

Customer: "I am buying a brand-new Toyota, so I have nothing to worry about."

F&I: "I agree Toyotas are wonderful cars, but let me ask you this: do you know that modern cars are not like the cars your parents drove. They have around 30,000 parts and basically are computers on wheels. The quality of Toyota's powertrain is legendary. When properly taken care of, those cars can go hundreds of thousands of miles. But what about all other components – electric seats, heated seats, navigation, laser cruise control, back-up camera, etc.? Would it make sense to have all these components covered for the next 6 years? Not to mention that this vehicle service contract covers towing, rental, and you can use it any licensed service facility in the country to do the repairs."

Gap Insurance Word Tracks

It Is Too Expensive

Customer: "I can't afford Gap."

F&I: "I hear you loud and clear. But let me ask you a crazy question, can you afford $5,500?"

Customer: "Of course not!"

F&I: "I want to share something with you—an average Gap claim right now is $5,500. In other words, customers without Gap coverage must pay this amount to the lender to satisfy the loan in case of a total loss. Would it make a better financial sense to pay an additional $20 per month and have this piece of mind?"

Gap From My Insurance Company is Cheaper

Customer: "I can get it for less from insurance company."

F&I: "Consider this: if you total your car, and your insurance policy and Gap are from the same the company, then you would have to file two claims. The first claim is for the accident and the second for Gap insurance. Guess what that would do to your monthly premium?"

Customer: "It would go up."

F&I: "Exactly. Would it make a better financial sense to pay an additional $20 per month and have this piece of mind?"

Gap From My Insurance Company is Cheaper #2

Customer: "I can get it for less from insurance company."

F&I: "No question about it. Keep in mind that you get what you pay for. Do you know what happens to Gap insurance if you decide to switch to a different insurance company because you found a better deal? You will lose your Gap coverage and be left without this valuable protection. So with that in mind, would it make a better financial sense to pay an additional $20 per month and have this piece of mind?"

Gap From My Insurance Company is Cheaper #3

Customer: "I can get it for less from my insurance company."

F&I: "I hear this all the time but let me ask you this: do you know that majority of Gap policies through insurance companies only go up to 115 percent loan to value whereas our Gap policy goes up to 150 percent. Imagine going through a total loss, a very stressful time in anybody's life, only to find out that your Gap policy didn't satisfy the loan in full. This would never happen with our Gap. Would it make a better financial sense to pay an additional $20 per month and have this piece of mind?"

Gap From My Insurance Company is Cheaper #4

Customer: "I can get it for less from insurance company."

F&I: "Yu are not wrong. But let me ask you this: do you know that most Gap policies through insurance companies do not cover negative equity from a previous loan that is rolled into a new loan. You are trading in a car that has negative equity, so this is a very important point to understand. This would never happen with our Gap. With that in mind, would it make a better financial sense to pay an additional $20 per month and have this piece of mind?"

Fixed Versus Variable Payment for Ancillary Products

Like with the vehicle service contract, a finance manager should use the fixed versus the variable payment to promote ancillary products.

F&I: "I understand that tire and wheel protection could be out of your budget, but imagine the following scenario: you hit a pothole and blow out two tires and bend two rims. The cost to replace both tires and rims is $1,200 plus another $100 for towing. Your base payment of $550 payment would go up to $1850 during that month. You see how your monthly payment is variable instead of being fixed?

"On the other hand, purchasing the tire and wheel protection is the guarantee that your monthly payment is fixed no matter what type of road hazard you encounter. Remember this tire and wheel protection plan covers tires, rims, cosmetic damage. It even covers all the taxes and towing. I am sure that you don't like surprises that could hurt your financially. Paying additional $22 per month for a tire and wheel protection plan will provide you with a true fixed payment. Does that make sense to you?"

I Am Not Buying Anything

Every finance manager has heard this before.

Customer: "I am not buying anything. Don't waste your time."

There's no need to be discouraged. Use the following word track to regain control.

F&I: "Not a problem. I understand. Let's review the free factory warranty that comes with your vehicle."

Customer: "Sounds good to me."

This is the opportunity for the finance manager to review and compare the factory comprehensive and powertrain warranty to the term of the loan. For example, if the customer is financing the vehicle for 72 months and the comprehensive warranty is 3 years or 36,000 miles and powertrain warranty is 5 years or 60,000 miles whichever comes first, it will become obvious to the customer that there are long periods of exposure. The finance manager should explain that the manufacturer's warranty doesn't cover tires and wheels, key, exterior and interior. Use the following word track to get back into the menu presentation.

F&I: "Now that you know what factory warranty covers, I am a little surprised that you didn't want to look at some of the protection packages that we offer. We have plans that start as low as $1 per day."

These are just a few examples of word tracks that work. Professional superstar finance managers work on improving their word tracks on a regular basis. Their word tracks reflect current events. For example, in a time with a high rate of inflation, we know that the parts and labor costs will go up across the country. A good finance manager will use the current state of economy to help the customer make the right choice. For example:

F&I: "By choosing to purchase the vehicle service contract, you are locking down the labor and parts costs. It doesn't matter if the costs will go up in the future. Your car is fully covered with a zero deductible."

In addition, superstar finance managers roleplay daily because they understand that delivery matters. Oftentimes, it is not what you say, it is how you say it. Roleplaying helps improve word tracks and focus on the tonality. Remember, every little detail matters. Al Pacino's character in the movie *Any Given Sunday* said it best:

"You find out life's this game of inches, so is football. Because in either game – life or football – the margin for error is so small. I mean, one half a step too late or too early and you don't quite make it. One half second too slow, too fast, and you don't quite catch it."

Best Practices

Finally, we can all learn from others. Over the years, excellent financial managers have developed best practices that, if followed, can lead to enormous success. I have detailed them in this book. Here is a summary:

- Focus on customer satisfaction
- Use Menus
- Use evidence manuals and visual aids
- Participate in regular training and role playing
- Keep current with technology
- Stay in compliance
- Review procedures on a regular basis
- Create standards and reward achievement.

CONCLUSION

I want to thank you for reading this book. As the front-end profit bonanza of 2020-2023 is coming to a logical end, the importance of F&I becomes more obvious. Remember that prior to the pandemic and the resulting inventory shortage, you couldn't run a successful dealership without a profitable F&I department. After reading this book, you are now on the path to professional, compliant and profitable F&I department.

Please do not hesitate to contact me with all your F&I income-development questions. My phone is always on, and I actually answer it.

917-903-0312
max@maxzanan.com

Printed in Great Britain
by Amazon

42062409R00057